TWAYNE'S WORLD AUTHORS SERIES

A Survey of the World's Literature

sity

JOSE SANTOS CHOCANO

by

PHYLLIS WHITE RODRIGUEZ-PERALTA

.José Santos Chocano is a Peruvian poet whose spectacular fame reversed itself within his lifetime. This book discusses Chocano's poetry from his first publications in 1895 through his posthumous volumes of 1939-1941. Avoiding the extremes of many critiques, the author presents both the strength and the defects of the poet's work. The assessment of Chocano's rightful place in Latin American literature probes the reasons for the adulation and the bitter criticisms which assailed the poet, particularly in his own Peru. Chocano's flamboyant life, so entwined with his poetry, is seen in the perspective of his own era. The chapter on Modernism traces the development of this movement in Spanish America, with special emphasis on Peru, and carefully considers the similarities and the differences between Chocano and the other Modernists. Several of Chocano's poems are translated and appear after the original Spanish.

and most of her writings center on Peruvian authors. She has been on the faculties of the University of Illinois, the University of Michigan, and, at present,of Temple University.

TWAYNE'S WORLD AUTHORS SERIES (TWAS)

*The purpose of TWAS is to survey the major writers
—novelists, dramatists, historians, poets, philosophers,
and critics—of the nations of the world. Among the
national literatures covered are those of Australia,
Canada, China, Eastern Europe, France, Germany,
Greece, India, Italy, Japan, Latin America, New Zea-
land, Poland, Russia, Scandinavia, Spain, and the
African nations, as well as Hebrew, Yiddish, and Latin
Classical literatures. This survey is complemented by
Twayne's United States Authors Series and English
Authors Series.*

*The intent of each volume in these series is to present a
critical-analytical study of the works of the writer; to
include biographical and historical material that may be
necessary for understanding, appreciation, and critical
appraisal of the writer; and to present all materials in
clear, concise, English—but not to vitiate the scholarly
content of the work by doing so.*

José Santos Chocano

By PHYLLIS W. RODRÍGUEZ-PERALTA

Temple University

Twayne Publishers, Inc.   ::   New York

to the memory of my father,

THOMAS WHITE

Acknowledgments

It is a pleasure to thank my colleagues who were kind enough to read parts of my manuscript and to offer their valuable suggestions. I am particularly grateful to Professor Lawrence Kiddle of the University of Michigan, Professor Irving Rothberg of the University of Massachusetts, and Professor George Edberg and Professor Clement Motten of Temple University.

I am also indebted to the librarians of the Interlibrary Loan Service of Temple University Libraries for their unfailing help which enabled me to use many original editions of Chocano's works. The Hispanic Society of America has also been most helpful.

Finally, I wish to thank my husband for his generous assistance in the preparation of this book.

Edna W. Underwood. *Spirit of the Andes*. (Portland, Maine: The Mosher Press, 1935): "The Arab Steeds of the Conquerors," "Spirit of the Andes," "The Puna."

University of Pennsylvania Press. Alice Stone Blackwell, *Some Spanish-American Poets* (1937): "Archaeology," "Sun and Moon," "The Volcanos," "The Magnolia."

JOSE SANTOS CHOCANO

Preface

JOSÉ SANTOS CHOCANO is a literary figure who kindles sharp emotion. Few poets have reaped the spectacular adulation that belonged to him during most of his lifetime; few poets have reaped the hostile invectives and abuse that fell on him during his last years. Extremes have followed him in the critiques, ranging from the glowing acclaim that lasted into the middle 1920's, through the bitter disparagements that prevailed in the 1930's and part of the 1940's, to the subsiding scorn beginning in the 1950's. His own Peru has been his most vehement ally and detractor. In spite of the tremendous shift in critical opinion, no anthology of Spanish American poetry—particularly of the Modernist movement—ever omits the name and poetic work of José Santos Chocano.

This book is a discussion of Chocano's poetry from his first publications in 1895 through his posthumous volumes of 1939–41. I have approached his work without the entangling national and personal prejudices and emotions that have accompanied most of the critiques, and it is my hope that this will smooth the way for an impartial consideration of both the defects and the strength inherent in Chocano's poems.

The poet said: "I always compose my verse after I have lived it." This complete entwining of Chocano's life with his poetry is responsible for the rather extensive chapter on his life. But there is another, more compelling reason for my seeming insistence on biographical material. Chocano was the culmination of the flavor of his own era, and he represented most fully the last vestiges of that seething world of late nineteenth-century Spanish America which spilled over into the first quarter of this century. Most of the bitter criticism and hatred which Chocano received, particularly from his own countrymen, originated in a generation which was struggling to free itself from exactly what Chocano represented. It seems to me that Chocano's work gains in interest and in understanding when seen in the perspective of his own time.

I have considered all of Chocano's poetic works, with an emphasis on the most characteristic facets of his art as they unfold and as they apply to his title "Poet of America." There is much confusion in the publications after 1908, compounded by the fact that a great portion of Chocano's poetry was published posthumously in an atmosphere of hostility or complete indifference. For these reasons, I have pointed out the original dates of publication whenever possible, and the constant revisions and alterations from one collection to another. On the other hand, I have commented only briefly on Chocano's prose, because the poet is so superior to the prose writer.

Editorial policy has specified that quotations be translated into English, and I have conformed to this policy in a number of ways—but always with regret for the drab black-and-white prints that are such a contrast to the vivid and glistening brush strokes of the originals. No translation can ever capture a poet's shimmering elusiveness nor faithfully transpose his art from one language to another. Nevertheless, I have made several translations of Chocano's poems, which appear after the original poetry, or I have used prose translations of pertinent, isolated lines in the poems. Occasionally I have been able to insert translations already made by other writers. The titles of Chocano's books and poems, when they are mentioned for the first time, have an English translation in parenthesis. In the chapter devoted to Modernism and Chocano's place within this literary movement, I found it necessary to retain some lines of poetry in the original Spanish in order to illustrate certain aspects of the poet's style.

In this discussion of Chocano's work I have attempted to assess his rightful place in Latin American literature, which I see as neither on the highest nor the lowest rung of true literary achievement. Much of his poetic work will disappear, like the fading America of his own era, but his best poems will always remain in the shining annals of Spanish American poetry. Each reader must, of course, form his own opinion. Whatever that opinion may be, it is my belief that Chocano's poetry deserves to be read in a new light, without preconceived views and in a spirit of impartiality.

P. R-P.

Contents

Chronology

1875   José Santos Chocano born in Lima, Peru, May 14.

1879– War of the Pacific; Chocano's childhood filled with scenes of
1883   war and the occupation of Lima by Chilean troops.

1884   Family moved to Chorrillos, sea resort near Lima.

1884– Began writing poetry sometime before age ten. At fifteen
1891   given editorship of one issue of respected literary journal.

1891– Studied at University of San Marcos.
1893

1893– Wrote inflammatory verses against dictatorial government
1894   of General Cáceres.

1894– To avoid political persecution prepared to flee country, but
1895   was seized. Faced firing squad; last-minute reprieve saved
his life. Became political prisoner until March, 1895.

1895– Put in charge of State Press. Published first two books of
1899   poetry: *Iras santas* (Holy Wrath, 1895) and *En la aldea*
(In the Village, 1895). Launched successive literary journals
and began a daily newspaper. Married Consuelo Bermúdez
in 1896. *Azahares* (Orange Blossoms, 1896). Made first trip
into interior of Peru. *Selva virgen* (Virgen Forest, 1898?).
La epopeya del Morro (The Epic of the Morro, 1899) and
El Derrumbe (The Debacle, 1899). Collaborated in literary
journals of America.

1900– Named special commissioner to Central American Republics
1903   to solicit votes in favor of compulsory arbitration. Became
Consul General in Central America. *El canto del siglo* (Song
of the Century, 1901) and *El fin de Satán y otros poemas*
(The End of Satan, and Other Poems, 1901). *Poesías
completas* (Complete Poems, 1902).

1903– Named chargé d'affaires in Bogotá. Had falling out with
1905   Prime Minister Pardo and resigned post. *Los cantos del
Pacífico* (Songs of the Pacific, 1904). Became agent of

Nicaraguan government; passed through Lima. Discontinued position and was named Secretary of Special Mission to king of Spain for arbitration of Peru's frontier dispute with Ecuador.

1905– Set out for Europe via southern countries of South America.
1908 Arrived in Madrid. *Alma América* (Soul of America, 1906) received lavish acclaim. Hailed as "Poet of America." Literary reputation at highest point. *¡Fiat Lux!* (Let there be Light,! 1908). Hasty departure from Madrid because of legal accusations.

1908– Arrived in Havana. In economic straits. Went to New
1912 York. Estrada Cabrera invited him to Guatemala. Founded *La Prensa* there. Obtained divorce and married Margot Batres Jáuregui.

1912– Arrived in Mexico as friend of Madero. At his assassination
1918 (1913) Chocano was taken prisoner and expelled from Mexico. Spent some time in Cuba. Visited Puerto Rico. *Puerto Rico lírico* (Lyric Puerto Rico, 1914?). Became agent of Carranza. Returned to Mexico. Was with Pancho Villa from 1915 to 1918. *Sumario del programa de la revolución mexicana* (Summary of the Program of the Mexican Revolution, 1915).

1919– Returned to Guatemala. Continued close friendship with
1921 dictator Estrada Cabrera. At his fall (1920) Chocano was sentenced to be executed. Saved by cables from king of Spain, two presidents, and ten congresses. Set free. In Costa Rica for several months.

1921– Returned to Peru, December, 1921. Triumphant recitals.
1924 *Idearium tropical* (Tropical Ideas, 1922). "Coronation" as Poet Laureate of Peru on November 5, 1922. Traveled through many Latin American countries giving recitals. *Ayacucho y los Andes* (Ayacucho and the Andes, 1924).

1925 Became embroiled in ideological disputes with various groups, descending to personal level with Edwin Elmore. On October 31, in the midst of heated argument, Chocano shot Elmore, who died two days later.

1925– Prisoner in Hospital Militar, October, 1925, to December,
1928 1927. Dramatic legal proceedings. Found guilty, June, 1926. Congress approved a law of amnesty. Freed in December, 1927. *El libro de mi proceso* (My Trial, 1927–28). With third

wife, Margarita Aguilar Machado, left Lima in November, 1928.

1928– Lived in Santiago, Chile. Collected and rewrote poetic
1934 material of many years. *Primicias de oro de Indias* (First Fruits from the Gold of the Indies, 1934). To relieve severe economic stress had many schemes for finding hidden treasure.

1934 December 13, stabbed to death in a streetcar by assailant indirectly involved in treasure hunts. Buried in borrowed mausoleum in Santiago, Chile.

1937– Posthumous works: *Poemas del amor doliente* (Poems of a
1941 Suffering Love, 1937). *Memorias. Las mil y una aventuras* (Memoirs. The Thousand and One Adventures, 1940). *El alma de Voltaire y otras prosas* (The Soul of Voltaire and Other Prose, 1940). *Oro de Indias* (The Gold of the Indies, four volumes, 1939, 1940, 1941).

1965 May. Peruvian government brought back his body for burial in native country.

CHAPTER 1

A Thousand and One Adventures

THE life of Chocano moves so swiftly and is so blatantly dramatic that it seems a swashbuckling, Romantic novel or a cape-and-sword theater piece. It is essential to know this life well, for Chocano's poetry blossomed out of his exuberant existence. Indeed his life and his writings are so entwined that one often reflects the other.

Chocano is actually a resume of an entire period in Latin America. In his memoirs he says: "My childhood is the War of the Pacific. My adolescence is the Spanish American War. I have been part of the beginning of Panamericanism, of the armed conflicts of Central America, of the Independence of Panama, of the intervention of the United States in Cuba, of the fall of Zelaya, of the Mexican Revolution—from the assassination of Madero to the assassination of Carranza. [I have been present] at the fall of Estrada Cabrera, at the Centennial of the Battle of Ayacucho, and finally, as if closing the circle with which the War of the Pacific opened my childhood, at the celebration of the Treaty on Tacna and Arica.... Death has had me waiting twice for the firing squad.... Three prisons have made me the central point of three circles in Dante's inferno."[1] Chocano's words describe only segments of his adventurous and multicolored existence, a mixture of vigor, audacity, and the picaresque.

José Santos Chocano was born in Lima, Peru, on May 14, 1875.

His father, José Félix Chocano de Zela, was an army captain from Tacna, in the south of Peru; his mother, María Aurora Gastañodi de la Vega, was born in Otuzco, a mountain town of the north near Trujillo. Chocano describes his father as martial and taciturn and his mother as energetic and vivacious, and he adds that in spite of their great disparity of temperament he never remembers the least disagreement between them. He was the second child, as the family included an older sister, María Virginia. His father died in 1909, when the poet was in Guatemala and at the height of his American prestige. His mother died in 1931, three years before her son's death in Chile.

The poet was intensely proud of his heritage. Through his father's family he could trace his direct descent from the illustrious Don Gonzalo Fernández de Córdoba, known in Spain as "The Great Captain." The family coat-of-arms bears the motto which Chocano proudly proclaimed as his own: "O encuentro camino o me lo abro" (Either I find a way or I make one). His great-grandfather was Francisco María de Zela, honored in Peru for raising the first cry of Peruvian independence against the Spanish, at Tacna, in 1811. His father was a captain in a later conflict between Peru and Spain, and he served with distinction in the final battle at Callao, 1866, when Spain bombarded the fortress of Real Felipe. His mother was the daughter of a wealthy Spanish miner. The ancestors of his father were Andalusian, and his maternal grandfather was a Basque. Chocano also states in his *Memorias* (Memoirs) that he supposes there is some Indian blood on both sides of his family.[2]

I *Historical Background of His Youth*

Lima is an elegant and aristocratic city; but it has always been ceremonious and frivolous, spiced with courtly intrigue and ironic laughter. A people who live in jest must expect tragedy. When Chocano was born, this tragedy had not yet struck, but it was imminent.

In 1875, the year of Chocano's birth, Peru was filled with unrest. Two sides represented opposite trends in political thinking. One was the Partido Civil, whose leader was Manuel Pardo; the other, the Partido Demócrata, was headed by Nicolás de Piérola. The pugnacity of these two parties created a climate of deep civic agitation throughout the country.

Meanwhile there were exterior threats to Peru, principally—from the Peruvian standpoint—the continued Chilean encroachments in the desert of Atacama. An alarmed Peru and Bolivia signed a treaty of defensive alliance in 1873. In February of 1879, Chile occupied the Bolivian port of Antofagasta in a dispute over Bolivia's right to levy an export tax on nitrates, and on April 5, war was declared on Peru.

Chocano was four when the War of the Pacific began. It was a bitter, desperate war, in which Peru suffered greatly. Lima was occupied for almost three years by Chilean troops, with serious harm to the city and its cultural institutions, culminating in the looting of the university and the destruction of the National Library.

The first boyhood heroes for Chocano were the Peruvian leaders in the War of the Pacific. The first stories he remembered were about the deeds of Nicolás de Piérola. Chocano says, "I was not able to be a child. I was prematurely a man. How could I scamper joyously through the fields when I might step into a pool of blood? How could I sing if my voice was to be drowned out by the metallic thunder of the cannon and the whistling of bullets?"[3]

He always retained the sharp, painful memory of his father leaving to fulfill his duty, while he and his sister clung to their silent mother. The desperate Battle of Miraflores took place at the doors of Lima, and a small boy could hear the pounding of the cannons and could not fail to see the streetcars bringing back the bloody bodies.

Tragedy swirled about his household, as it did everywhere in Peru. President Prado had left Peru for Europe, supposedly to secure aid. There was a boiling over of civil treasons in which political passions dislodged patriotism. There were political intrigues even on the front lines facing the enemy.

Chile was victorious, and the occupation of Lima began when Chocano was almost six. He says that the trumpets of the conquering army deafened his childhood forever. In that captive city he remained a prisoner too, behind the walls of his home, with books instead of playmates to relieve the tedium and silence of the house. When peace came, Chocano was no longer a little boy.

In 1883 Peru was forced to accept the Chilean terms, but the Chilean soldiers were not withdrawn from Peruvian territory until 1884, when the treaty was ratified. Chile imposed: unconditional cession in perpetuity of Peru's nitrate province of Tarapacá; and possession of the provinces of Tacna and Arica for a period of ten years, after which a plebiscite would decide whether the territory was to remain under the Chilean flag or revert to Peru.

The country recovered slowly from this harsh conflict and remained crippled economically, politically, and culturally for a long period.

II   *After the War*

Chocano was nine when the occupation of Lima ended. His father moved the family to Chorrillos, a picturesque resort on the Pacific Ocean where fashionable *limeños* spent their summers. In 1881, Chorrillos had been the scene of a raging battle, and more than half the town lay in rubble over which new houses were built. The verses of one of his first books, *En la aldea* (In the Village), would come out of the whitewashed peace of a seashore.

Chocano studied first in the Colegio Alemán and then in the Colegio de Lima,[4] a secondary school. His capacity for mathematics was quite evident and led his mother to plan a career for him as an engineer. He received the Gold Medal for scholastic excellence, and the Colegio de Lima asked him to serve on its faculty as an instructor in mathematics.

In 1891, just before his sixteenth birthday, he took the entrance examinations for the respected and traditional University of San Marcos, and enrolled in the Faculty of Letters. It was a brief stop, over by 1893. Chocano says that his individualism, fostered by the solitude of his childhood and the accompanying smell of gunpowder, had made him into a combative adolescent, impatient with the oppressive atmosphere of the university. Whether this is rationalization or insight, Chocano's opinion of the university is unmistakable. His *Memorias* contain a scathing denunciation of the mediocrity he found in that "arena of incompetent instruction."

Other fields beckoned to him, and with youthful impatience he rushed to take part in the opposition against the dictatorial government of General Andrés Avelino Cáceres. Fiery protests, verses saturated with rebellion, were published in *La Tunda* (a liberal weekly) and signed with the pseudonym "Juvenal."

Like most Latin American poets, Chocano had begun writing verse early in his life, certainly before ten. Around fourteen to fifteen years of age he often used the pseudonym "Bíbolo" to sign his manuscripts of poetic collections which he apparently tried to publish, without success. In January, 1891, when he was fifteen, he was given the editorship of one special issue of *El Perú Ilustrado*, a respected literary journal. This stroke of good fortune for such a young person came about because of a bitter ideological dispute involving the clergy and traditionalists opposed to the directors of the journal, which in turn caused the controversial author Clorinda

Matto de Turner to leave her post as editor.[5] In that same year Chocano's work appeared in the literary journal *Fin de Siglo*; next he collaborated in the journals *La Idea* and *La Razón* of Lima. In 1892, he published an article on the Mexican poet Salvador Díaz Mirón for the journal *El Progresista* of Arequipa. A portrait of Chocano appeared in an 1893 issue of *El Perú Artístico*, next to his poem "El sermón de la montaña" (The Sermon on the Mount), in which he does not mind mingling his own protests with the words of Christ.

Thus the young poet was not unknown in his country, which made it fairly easy to guess the identity of the "Juvenal" who was writing the inflammatory verses in *La Tunda* (1893-94). The tyrannical government of Cáceres was hardly the type to respect the lyre, especially if it was vibrating insults, and suddenly Chocano made hurried preparations to leave the country.

He was filled with premonitions as he and a friend made their way to the docks of Callao, but the urgency to escape overcame his distrust of the stevedore who had arranged the incognito passages. Intrigue and secrecy and fear were a necessary part of that Peruvian atmosphere. But the stevedore was a spy who had betrayed them! Suddenly they were surrounded by a dozen armed policemen and taken to police headquarters in Callao. No calls were allowed. The frightening fact was that no one knew the poet's whereabouts nor his plans. There was a guard who came to tell Chocano how much he admired his poetry, and he even agreed to send a telegram to Chocano's family in Lima. The poet doubted the offer. He and his friend were made to walk through the dark, deserted streets to the police station at Bellavista, and there they were tied and led out near the sea to be shot. In the midst of this anguishing experience the chief of police appeared. They were untied and sent back to headquarters.

The next morning Chocano's father was allowed a few minutes with his son, sufficient time to tell him of the urgent pleas of the night past. The guard who had liked Chocano's poetry had actually sent the telegram, and the combined efforts of the archbishop and the authorities in Lima had saved the poet's life.

With other political prisoners Chocano was sent to the subterranean dungeons of the Real Felipe in Callao and forced to endure incredible prison conditions.[6] His indomitable spirit arose, and full of violence and anger he retaliated with flaming verses

which would be his *Iras santas* (Holy Wrath), in which he shouted
that he would incarcerate his jailers in the prison of his verses and
his lyre would be their bars.

In March, 1895, Piérola entered Lima. After a bloody conflict
of two days the Diplomatic Corps succeeded in arranging a truce
to bury the dead, and during this time Cáceres disappeared
mysteriously from the Government Palace. A Junta was formed,
joining the irreconcilable adversaries of former years. Manuel
Candamo, of the Civilista party, presided over the Junta, but
Piérola, of the opposite party, was soon elected president. The
coalition Cívico-demócrata revolution had triumphed.

Chocano left prison on this wave of triumph. He became the
private secretary of Candamo and Elías Malpartida, minister of the
treasury, the two of opposing parties. This was not the position
Chocano wanted, and soon he was put in charge of the State Press,
which he succeeded in transforming into a cooperative. It was 1895
and he was twenty.

III   The Years 1895–1900

The next five years were an epoch of febril activity for the poet.
In 1895, the State Press published his first two books of poetry:
Iras santas, fruit of his imprisonment, and *En la aldea*, animistic
verses from his life in Chorrillos.[7] Here are two opposing facets of
the poet's spirit, each essential for a complete understanding of his
work. *Iras santas* burst upon the Peruvian scene with tremendous
force. The entire nation was moved by the flaming lines which
served somehow to restore national pride still shattered from the
Chilean defeat. In addition, the small group which made up the
cultured elite applauded the new forms of poetry still comparatively unused in Peru. *Iras santas* was published in red letters to
emphasize the poet's anger; *En la aldea* appeared in blue, perhaps to
suggest the tranquillity of the Peruvian coast. In both there is the
flavor of Spanish America. One measures the pulse of an Hispanic
revolution; the other is the breath of the sea air and the countryside
near Lima.

As director of the State Press, Chocano was able to launch
successive editorial projects: *El Perú Ilustrado* (1895), which
became *La Neblina* (1896–97), and then *La Gran Revista* (1897). At
the end of 1897, he conceived the idea of a great daily newspaper
which would make journalistic strides for Lima. Thus *Siglo XX* was

born, a newspaper which lasted several months, with two daily editions and multiple innovations in typographical presentation.

Chocano's attempts at drama received little applause. His first play appeared in 1896, a short-lived work originally entitled *El hombre sin mundo* (The Man without a World) but frequently cited in bibliographical listings as *Sin nombre* (Without Name). Another play in 1900, called *Vendimiario* (First Month), was also a failure.

In 1896, he married Consuelo Bermúdez, daughter of a colonel who had died in the recent revolution. His third book of verse, *Azahares* (Orange Blossoms, 1896), was inspired by this love and is a sentimental and youthful offering. (In his *Memorias* Chocano bluntly advises that no young girl, except one bent on being a martyr, should marry a poet of twenty-one, especially a poet who wishes to devote his life to living his poetry.)

The first edition of *Selva virgen* probably appeared in 1896 also, although the date 1898 is usually given, with successive and augmented versions during the next few years. In these poems the author roams through various styles and subjects, and he takes many steps within the contemporary movement of Modernism. The title was suggested by his trip to the valley of Chanchamayo where—always optimistically enterprising—he had hoped to begin a vast coffee plantation. A few of the poems in this collection show certain pictorial aspects of nature, indicating the effect of this first contact with the mountains and the jungles, but the full consequences unfolded in his next works.

Perhaps nothing had such direct impact upon Chocano's subsequent poetry as this first trip out of the environs of the capital. Lima is a city without snow, without rain, without thunder or lightning, without well-defined seasons, without great heat or great cold. It is a city given to elegance and ceremony. Imagine, then, the intensity of emotion which Chocano would experience on his first trip into the magnificent interior of Peru. The poet of Lima was stunned by the vast silence of the cordillera, by its sepulchral eternity. He saw the mountains as bodies of heroes writhing desperately but in silence, their anguish betrayed only by a tear running into the rivers below. He sensed strength and melancholy as the two psychic notes of the Andes. He imagined a primitive tragedy in which the forces of nature, personified in inaccessible peaks, abysmal depths, and gushing rivers, would clash against the

tyranny of human creativeness, triumphant in the solemn desecra-
tion of a train. This train crossing successive tunnels through the
snow-capped peaks suggested a needle that would sew mountains
together. All these images were set down in his later poetry. He saw
his first storm. He heard the musical lament of the *quena* (Indian
flute) that wept for the past glory of a conquered race. Three days
on horseback brought him into the *selva*, the Peruvian jungles, and
the lush, twisted and wild flora and fauna indelibly marked his
spirit. When the poet returned to his native Lima it was with a
dream of poetry which he felt would be truly American, and all his
subsequent verse shows the stamp of these impressions.

In 1899, he had two poetic triumphs which increased his stature
as an inspired poet in America: *El Derrumbe* (The Debacle) and
La epopeya del Morro (The Epic of the Morro). *El Derrumbe* surged
out of his inspiration before the great Peruvian *selva* (and is an
indication of the poetry that will come to full flower in *Alma
América* [Soul of America]). Set with passages of spontaneous
beauty and power, we have Chocano's first romanticized vision of
the Indian. *La epopeya del Morro* is one of his greatest epic poems.
It reflects the deeds of the Peruvian hero Francisco Bolognesi and
the Peruvian cavalry, who preferred to die rather than surrender to
the Chilean troops.

Old wounds had opened in Peru in these years. According to the
terms of the treaty with Chile, a plebiscite should have been held in
1894 to decide the definitive fate of the provinces of Tacna and
Arica. The situation had not been resolved, and within this climate
Chocano conceived his poem *La epopeya del Morro*. This work set
Chocano definitely in the direction he was to follow in his epic
poetry. The spirit of solidarity sweeping over Spanish America as
a result of the war between the United States and Spain, and later
events in his own life, caused him to widen his epic vision to include
all of Latin America.

During this period of intense literary creation Chocano's work
appeared in the literary journals of the entire continent, including
all the well-known Modernist journals: in Mexico, *La Revista
Azul*, founded by Manuel Gutiérrez Nájera and Carlos Díaz Dufóo,
and *La Revista Moderna*, founded by Amado Nervo and Jesús
Valenzuela; *La Lira Chilena* and *Pluma y Lápiz* of Santiago;
La Montaña of Buenos Aires, under the direction of Leopoldo
Lugones and José Ingenieros; in Bogotá, *La Revista Gris*, directed

by Max Grillo; *La Revista Ilustrada* and *Las Tres Américas* of New York; *El Fígaro* and *La Habana Elegante* of Cuba; and in Caracas, *El Cojo Ilustrado*. It is clear that Chocano always sought to keep himself apart from strict adherence to the rules of Modernism as practiced by the Spanish American coterie of the new literature.

IV New Directions: 1900–1905

The twentieth century had arrived. Chocano's life and his incessant creative activity continued at the same vigorous pace. In 1900–1901 he collaborated in *El Modernismo*, edited by his friend Domingo Martínez Luján. His *El canto del siglo* (Song of the Century) appeared in 1901, a presumptuous tribute to the past century and the new era.

It seems fairly certain that by this point in his career Chocano had determined to make himself the poet of the American scene. Undoubtedly he felt that he should gravitate in this direction because it offered the best possibilities for wide recognition.

The poet had not progressed at the same rate in either his finances or in politics. Always intrigued with power, Chocano had given his suggestions upon numerous occasions, but his gifts as author were more in demand than his advice. In 1901, the situation changed. At that time Peru was vitally concerned with lining up votes in favor of the doctrine of compulsory arbitration, an issue which would be debated at the Second Panamerican Conference to be held in Mexico, 1901–1902. President Eduardo López Romaña named Chocano as Peru's special commissioner (without official title) to the Central American republics, with the hope that he could influence these countries to promise their votes in favor of Peru's position.

Chocano's life of incessant travel began with this voyage. From then on he would return to Peru for only brief periods. Instead, the world would be the arena for his thousand and one adventures.

Leaving Callao, he stopped in Ecuador, Panama (still part of Colombia), Costa Rica, and Guatemala. He absorbed the diverse landscapes of the Americas, and indeed the beauty of the tropics had a deep and lasting influence on his poetry. He also crystallized his idea that there should be no barriers among nations so closely bound together by the ties of language, history, and cultural background.

Chocano's literary fame had preceded him, and at each stop admiring authors came to greet him. When he installed himself with pomp in Guatemala, the writers gathered around him, and no doubt he spoke to them with olympic grandeur. President Manuel Estrada Cabrera, who ruled Guatemala with an iron hand, sent his greetings. A strong friendship developed between these two men, with the immediate result that Estrada Cabrera promised Guatemala's vote for the Peruvian position. (Chocano always insisted that he had not sought out the friendship with Estrada Cabrera, but the other way around.) As a gesture of appreciation for so much admiration, Chocano decided to publish *El fin de Satán y otros poemas* (The End of Satan, and Other Poems) in Guatemala, in 1901.

From Lima he received broad hints to get on with his mission. Returning to give an account of his activity, Chocano assured everyone that of the five Central American votes he was sure of three in favor of the Peruvian thesis of compulsory arbitration.[8] President López Romaña was pleased and named him consul-general in Central America, a position he held until 1903.

Meanwhile his *Poesías completas* (Complete Poems) had been published in Barcelona, early in 1902, with a prologue by Manuel González Prada. Chocano felt deep admiration for this great Peruvian liberal and had made overtures of friendship when González Prada returned from Europe in 1898. The latter, for his part, had been favorably impressed by Chocano's *Iras santas* and *En la aldea*. However, González Prada opposed Piérola, and since Chocano was his ardent champion there was bound to be a certain personal reserve between the two. It was probably a desire for conciliation which prompted Chocano to ask González Prada to write the prologue to *Poesías completas*.

As consul-general, Chocano's residence was in Guatemala, and this time he sent for his wife. By now they had two sons, Eduardo Adolfo, born in December, 1897, and José Alberto, born in August, 1901. A third and last son, José Santos, was born in October, 1903. Soon after that Chocano's marriage to his first wife, Consuelo, came to an end.

In his new diplomatic capacity Chocano continued to enjoy excellent personal relations with the Guatemalan dictator Estrada Cabrera. In 1903 a border dispute flared up between Guatemala and El Salvador, apparently goaded by Estrada Cabrera's rival

José Santos Zelaya, dictator of Nicaragua. Provocative military activity disturbed the two countries, and war seemed inevitable. Chocano audaciously offered his good offices of friendship. With the blessing of Estrada Cabrera he traveled to El Salvador for an audience with the dictator, General Tomás Regalado, and as a result of this interview he succeeded in arranging a future conference on board ship. The leaders of the two countries met, reached an understanding, and war was averted.[9]

Chocano gave himself full credit for this outcome, and the entire continental press commented on the episode. The poet received letters of appreciation for his personal intervention from the presidents of Guatemala and El Salvador and the president-elect of Honduras, which were published in the presses of Peru and of Central America. Lima could not remain deaf, and in 1903, when the poet had returned home, he was named chargé d'affaires in Central America.

López Romaña was concluding his term of office in Peru, to be followed by the new president, Manuel Candamo. Chocano apparently felt that destiny had called him to intervene for his country, and he gave his advice freely as to the correct choice of ministers for the new government. According to Chocano, his suggestions were gratefully received and acted upon; thus, he was responsible for the appointments of José Pardo and Javier Prado Ugarteche, and in part, for Augusto Leguía. Actually in Peru the family name is more important than all else, and Candamo undoubtedly made his choices on that basis.

Cablegrams began to arrive with the news that an expedition from Nicaragua had disembarked in the Isthmus of Panama. Communications were poor and the situation not clear when a definitive cable was received claiming the Independence of Panama, attained by the aid of the government of the United States (November 3, 1903). Peru faced a dilema. Her interests dictated immediate recognition of Panama, for the United States had become involved in settling the dispute over Tacna and Arica. Opposed to this was the necessity of reaching an agreement with Colombia in regard to the Amazon limits. Peru decided upon recognition of Panama, thus running the risk of alienating the good will of Colombia. In these difficult circumstances Prime Minister Pardo changed Chocano's appointment and named him chargé d'affaires in Bogotá. A poet in a country of poets would be a good place for Chocano.

Leaving immediately, the poet passed through Panama during days of historical significance. In spite of the cloud over relations between Peru and Colombia, Chocano was received cordially in Bogotá. His youth and talent favored him, and the writers welcomed him in their midst. Naturally all this facilitated his mission. Shortly he cabled Lima that an agreement had been reached to submit the question of the Amazon boundaries to arbitration before the king of Spain. Apparently Chocano felt that the document must be concluded in Bogotá, with himself as the signer for Peru. After considerable delay a cable came from Peru insisting that the Colombian Chancery instruct its minister in Lima to sign the treaty there. Chocano felt that Pardo was using this diplomatic success for his own advantage and defended his right to sign the agreement in Bogotá. A falling out occurred between the two over this situation. Chocano cabled that if the treaty was to be signed in Lima, he would resign. An answering cable announced that Chocano was to follow orders and alluded to a possible loss of face for the poet-diplomat. Chocano was furious over what he believed was an insult delivered in an official cablegram, and he telegraphed his resignation.

Through all this turmoil Chocano continued his writing. In 1904, he authorized his first anthology, entitled *Los cantos del Pacífico* (Songs of the Pacific), published in Paris.

Casting about for new opportunities, he began to occupy himself with the project of a canal in Nicaragua, and he set out for that country to discuss his plans with Zelaya. He went by way of Costa Rica, and there he became involved in a duel because of some insults published against him. When he arrived in Nicaragua, Zelaya immediately offered his friendship. However, the dictator was apparently more interested in his own affairs than in the canal idea, and he persuaded Chocano to become a confidential agent of Nicaragua, based in Argentina.

The poet was delighted to pass through Lima on his way to Buenos Aires, probably to visit his parents and to arrange his own family affairs, and certainly to flaunt his importance in front of the politicians. Exactly what took place in Lima is not clear. Candamo had died a few months after assuming office, and José Pardo—because of the previous death of the first vice-president—had become the new president. Either personally, or possibly through Javier Prado, Pardo was sufficiently persuasive with Chocano so that instead of continuing his trip as Zelaya's confidential agent, the poet accepted another post. He was named secretary of the Special Mission being sent to the king of Spain for arbitration of the difficulties with Ecuador over the Amazon frontiers.

Chocano set out for Europe in 1905; he would not return to Peru for nearly seventeen years. Before embarking for Spain, the poet traveled through the southern countries of South America. By now Chocano's prestige was international, and his rebel spirit, very well known. His first stop was in Santiago, and as might have been expected there was some unpleasant publicity in Chile. After all, he was not only the author of *La epopeya del Morro*, but also the Peruvian representative who had advocated compulsory arbitration. Nevertheless, the good will of the writers far outshown the hostility. From Chile he crossed the Andean cordillera and arrived in Buenos Aires, where he was cordially received. Next came Montevideo, where he met the authors Julio Herrera y Reissig, Victor Pérez Petit, and Juan Zorrilla de San Martín. With his soul brimming over with poetry, he left Montevideo for Río de Janeiro.

Chocano's journey through these Latin American countries was of untold benefit to him. Until this time—in spite of his bravado a la Byron and Espronceda—the poet was really the provincial writer of *En la aldea*. The new horizons which opened before him in the southern countries and his contacts with well-known authors taught him a great deal and immeasurably enriched the pages of his poetry. In the Old World atmosphere of cultured Spain he would learn even more.

V   *The Madrid Years*

Undoubtedly Chocano expected to conquer Madrid as he had the Latin American capitals. But Chocano was only one of a great many poetic lights in the Spanish capital, among them the most famous of the Modernists. A common saying in the cafés was: "The latest first American poet has arrived in Madrid."[10] Chocano's facial expression was too theatrical and his posture too martial for the innately charming Spanish. His voice seemed too sonorous and stylized, his hair too black and too slicked down, his collars overly stiff, his mustache exaggeratedly waxed. Madrid smiled.

Spain, for Chocano, was profoundly impressive, and he eagerly drank in her beauty. Very quickly he became part of the world of Spanish letters. He conversed often with the renowned writer and philosopher, Miguel de Unamuno, and the critic and scholar, Marcelino Menéndez y Pelayo. He met many of the best-known Spanish authors and poets of the day, among them Pérez Galdós, Benavente, Valle Inclán, Pío Baroja, Pardo Bazán, Salvador Rueda, Antonio and Manuel Machado, Pérez de Ayala, Julio Camba, Villaespesa, "Azorín," Echegaray. He and Rubén Darío, the celebrated Modernist from Nicaragua, became intimate friends, allowing for the occasional cooling-off periods necessary for two poetic temperaments. (Chocano often tried to counterbalance Darío's bouts with alcohol, a vice which Chocano did not possess and which filled him with disdain.) The Mexican poet Amado Nervo was also among his good friends.

Chocano did not yet have the coveted blessing of the Ateneo, Madrid's hermetic literary society, but he managed to receive an invitation to recite his verses at a ceremony of homage to the deceased writer Francisco Navarro Ledesma.

All of literary Madrid was present. Chocano's newly composed poem "La elegía del órgano" (Elegy of the Organ) was written in onomatopoetic form in free verse. When Chocano began to recite, with his affected gravity of mien and his dramatic manner of speech, the audience was provoked to laughter. Three times he began "Suena el órgano" (The organ sounds), and the hilarity became more intense. Convinced of the beauty of his work, Chocano continued undaunted by the smirks and jests. Little by little the imaginative, eloquent metaphors and the flowing lines dominated the laughter, and when he finished, a thunderous ovation greeted him. The poet from America had triumphed, and he had gained the full respect of the writers of Madrid.

It was both his greatest achievement and his downfall. As he was a poet and a diplomat from Peru, he was supposed to be wealthy; there was always a chorus of adventurers around him. He was now an intimate of the Ateneo, and an avid member of Madrid café society. He was presented to Alfonso XIII, to whom he dedicated his *Alma América*, his first book published in Spain (1906).

In April, 1906, his drama *Los Conquistadores* (The Conquerors) opened. This venture in the theater had a very small measure of contemporary success and is never considered among the lasting contributions of Chocano. In the verses of this heroic drama Chocano attempted an interweaving of the Inca empire and Spain, the mother country—of the conquered and the conqueror.

Later in 1906 came his famous *Alma América*, the zenith of his literary creation. There are two nearly simultaneous first editions, one from Madrid and one from Paris. The Spanish version carries a prologue by Unamuno and a short letter from Menéndez y Pelayo, and both editions have a penetrating introductory poem by Rubén Darío. (In his *Memorias* Chocano says that a bottle of brandy brought about Darío's spontaneous poem.) A page of the poet's mottoes contains his personal creed, "Either I find a way or I make one," and as if to stress that he has acquired a new critical conscience he adds, "Consider as if not written those books which appeared before with my signature."

Alma América is a torrent of verse through which pass the Incas resplendent in their glory, the immense rivers of a Continent, the towering, gigantic peaks of the Andes, the condors proudly soaring above vast spaces, elegant viceroys, volcanos, old heraldic cities, millenary forests, jaguars, orchids, conquerors. This was the New World for the delighted Spanish audience. Chocano was the "Poet of America" who had crossed the Atlantic to offer his exotic songs. The Spanish critics were lavish with their acclaim of *Alma América*. At thirty-one Chocano's wildest dream had come true—he was regarded even in Spain as a great poet!

In Madrid his life became dramatic and colorful. He strode proudly through the streets, a flower in his buttonhole and a cane on his arm, his head arrogantly erect. Many were irritated with the self-satisfied poses, the imperious gestures, the obvious vanity. But these irritants disappeared in the pleasure of listening to him. Chocano must have considered himself a gift to creation, and he immediately plunged into many kinds of business ventures, all failures in spite of his self-esteem as a financier.

In 1908, his excellent *¡Fiat Lux!* (Let there be Light!) was published, again in Madrid and Paris. The earlier Spanish edition is hurried, with an omission of several poems which appear in the second Paris edition published later in the same year. *¡Fiat Lux!* contains new poetry, and in part is an anthology culled from his youthful poems, corrected and revised with exemplary severity. It ranks with *Alma América* at the peak of Chocano's work.

There was reason for the haste of the Spanish edition. Although the facts are not clear, even Chocano's detractors—and they are legion—seem to feel that at this point he was duped. Each biographer must make his own interpretation of the meager details available. Apparently someone involved Chocano in cashing a false check, seemingly authorized by the poet. His financier "friends" had abused his signature, but the Bank of Spain implacably charged the diplomat. The accusation of "swindler" went from mouth to mouth. The threat of legal action and imprisonment hung over the poet. Everything seemed to be against him. He fled the country.

In the wake of the scandal Darío is supposed to have made this statement: "American poetry can be proud of having the greatest assassin: Díaz Mirón; the greatest thief: Chocano; and the greatest drunkard: myself."[11] Whether Darío actually said this is an open question. Undoubtedly his pride had suffered at seeing such acclaim going to another American whom they called the "Poet of America," which might account for the caustic words. In addition, Darío did apparently accept Chocano's guilt, and it cost Chocano a great deal to forgive him in later years.

VI   *The Years in the Caribbean Countries, Central America, and Mexico*

Always violent and proud, Chocano reacted against Spain. Now he did not wish to recall his statements of her glory. All that was past, and the poet looked to new adventures. Yet his poem "Fin de raza" (Death of a Race), written in 1908, points up the bitterness he had tasted: "Legendary race, museum-piece country,/Spain is like a macabre vision."[12]

The return voyage to America was a difficult one. "Oda salvaje" (Savage Ode), apparently also from 1908, reveals the anguish of the poet: "I return to you with a healthy soul/in spite of sick civilizations. . . . Now that I have returned to you/I feel your sap in my veins."[13] He arrived in Havana in June, 1908, and found Cuba hospitable. Always an indefatigable worker, he published numerous poems in *El Fígaro*. He also directed the social page of *El diario de la Marina*, which reveals his obvious need for money.

In spite of the continued literary glory that was his after *Alma América* and *¡Fiat Lux!*, the preocupation of the lawsuit in Spain and the necessity of finding means to sustain himself weighed heavily upon the poet. His friends of that period found him pale and emaciated. The blow in Spain had been very hard, especially as evidence points more to his carelessness than to any fraud on his part.

In July, he traveled to the Dominican Republic, to be received in triumph. He returned to Havana; and apparently feeling a little more kindly toward Spain, he attended a farewell party for the crew of the Spanish ship *Nautilus* and dedicated a poem to that occasion. The Ateneo of Havana honored him. Everything seemed to be going well.

Then disturbing rumors came from Spain. The Bank of Spain was continuing the lawsuit against him and was attempting to ask for his extradition. Naturally, ugly gossip began to circulate in Havana. Meeting the situation head on, Chocano published an open letter to the Director of *El diario de la Marina* (dated September 21, 1908) in which he explained his side of the question. Adopting an attitude of injured pride, he accused the Bank of Spain of conspiring against his peace of mind and his honor.

Unfortunately, Chocano saw fit to leave Cuba immediately, bound for the United States under an assumed name. Most of the Cuban press was favorable to the poet, with the exception of precisely the *Diario de la Marina*, which published a stinging attack against Chocano in its September 25 edition.

The poet disembarked in New Orleans. When he was asked why he had traveled under a different name, he rather lamely explained that it was to avoid being questioned by the North American reporters, and that anyhow he wished to laugh at the extradition procedures going on in Spain, since he was far away from the legal situation.

He went by train to New York, an experience which brought forth several fine compositions. There was a rapid trip through Cuba in 1909, and then Estrada Cabrera invited him to Guatemala. There he founded *La Prensa*, and as usual, engaged in business ventures, this time in mining.

In Guatemala there was a new love, Margot Batres Jáuregui. Her parents were violently opposed to the match. Perhaps they had even met Chocano's legal wife when she had accompanied the poet to Guatemala in 1903. With much difficulty Chocano finally succeeded in obtaining a power of attorney from his wife Consuelo (there was no divorce in Peru), and he initiated successful divorce proceedings in Guatemala. Free to marry according to Guatemalan law, the wedding took place in New York, in 1912.

A letter to Darío, written around this period, speaks caustically of the reasons for his departure from Spain: "It is stupid to think that one can be humbled for offending the laws and customs, when one was born, not contrary, but superior to the laws."[14] Although

there was evident scar tissue, the resplendent, arrogant Chocano
had recovered completely.

Meanwhile the Mexican Revolution had exploded. Chocano had
been in contact with Francisco Madero, leader of the movement
against the dictator Porfirio Díaz. Apparently anxious to apply his
economic and political ideas, and always lured by action, Chocano
arrived in Mexico. Looking for new business ventures, he established a factory for making decorative paper. He moved in the
circle close to Madero and was in Mexico City when the army rose
against the president under the command of Victoriano Huerta.
President Madero was assassinated (1913). Soldiers soon surrounded
Chocano's hotel, making him a prisoner, and Huerta decreed the
immediate expulsion of that "pernicious foreigner" from Mexican
territory. Hastily he was put on board a ship bound for Germany—
but which docked in Havana.

It was 1913 and the poet was thirty-eight. Margot awaited him
in Guatemala. However, he spent some time in Cuba, where again
he was well received. He attempted to provoke protest in the
shadow of the tightening vigilance of the United States in the
Caribbean. Soon he became the agent of Venustiano Carranza of
Mexico, who was maintaining the latent spirit of resistance against
Huerta. He was invited to Puerto Rico and earned a considerable
amount of money from the many recitals he offered during his
two-month stay. On the island he gave two speeches of importance:
one a strong anti-imperialist discourse; and the other a farewell
speech to Puerto Rico in which he explained his literary views.
Later his *Puerto Rico lírico* (Lyric Puerto Rico) appeared (San
Juan, probably 1914), which contained new poetry and a prologue
by the poet Luis Llorrens Torres. In that same year a volume
of translated poems of the Brazilian A. Fontoura Xavier was
published, with José Santos Chocano as the translator. (A particularly exaggerated prologue by Chocano accompanies the work.)
Returning to Havana, he gave a speech in which he asked Washing-
ton not to recognize the government of Huerta.

Carranza sent for him, and he traveled to Mexico once more. In
1915, he was in the north, where he remained nearly three years at
the side of Francisco (Pancho) Villa during his rebel activities. For
Villa, Chocano edited *Sumario del programa de la revolución
mexicana* (Summary of the Program of the Mexican Revolution,

1915), and the poet soon came to be known as the "Word of the Revolution."[15]

Margot accompanied Chocano in Mexico, and apparently Villa greatly admired both the poet and his wife. There is a fascinating story told which illustrates the strange alliance of the poet and the *caudillo*. One night when Chocano was reciting his poems in Pancho Villa's bivouac, an aide dashed in with some important news concerning the troops. Without permitting him to continue, Villa drew out his pistol and fired at the unhappy man. The bullet whistled over the head of the astonished poet. Indignantly Villa announced, "When the poet Chocano recites, no one interrupts him."[16]

In 1918, there was a shift in the Mexican turmoil, and Chocano separated from Villa. His poem "Ultima rebelión" (The Last Rebellion, 1920?) is dedicated to the fallen leader. The Mexican adventure had ended for Chocano. Again he must begin anew. He still possessed his indomitable will and his continually flowing talent.

Chocano's poetry of this ten-year epoch mirrors his life of action (except for the work immediately after his return from Spain, when he seems momentarily deflated). One of his most famous lines, written early in this period, announces: "Walt Whitman has the North; but I have the South."[17] Around this idea spun all his production between 1908 and 1918. He strove consciously to be indeed the "Poet of America." In "Oda continental" (Ode for a Continent) he attempted a dazzling prediction of future continental glories, setting his prophecies in a Biblical meter often associated with Whitman. In order to put more distance between himself and the Modernism of Darío, he practiced what he had proclaimed in one of the mottoes of *Alma América*: "In Art all schools fit, as in a sunbeam, all the colors of the spectrum."

It was 1919, and Chocano was forty-four. World War I had ended. Once more Central America opened its doors to the poet when his old friend Estrada Cabrera invited him to Guatemala. It was said that the dictator handed over the monopoly of refined sugar to his new political adviser, and that all shippers had to go through the poet to obtain their merchandise. His enemies whispered that he obtained constant concessions from the dictator. His family and friends stressed his tranquil home life, his writing, his recitals.

Chocano seems to have been at peace with his surroundings in

Guatemala. (There had been two children born of his second marriage, a son, Alberto, and a daughter, María Angélica, in 1915 and 1917.) This was the time of new poetry, and of polishing his work, both published and unpublished.

In 1920 there was much talk of revolution and social justice. In the subsequent Guatemalan uprising, Estrada Cabrera was overthrown after nearly twenty-three years of rule. The rabble sacked the house of the poet, burning all his work in preparation, his notes, his papers. As the personal friend of the fallen dictator, Chocano was seized, imprisoned in a dungeon, and sentenced to be executed.[18] The lines from his poems written in prison accept bravely, and even proudly, the fate he expected.

His wife was allowed to pass to the border, and she moved the Spanish world with her pleas. Cables arrived in Guatemala from all over the world. The king of Spain, the presidents of Peru and Argentina, and the Congresses of ten Latin American countries interceded for the "Poet of America." The Junta Revolucionaria could not help but feel the weight of these demands, and the poet was set free. When his train was leaving for Costa Rica, his enemies alerted an intermediary station so that they would know who was on that train. By a stroke of luck the telegram was delayed, and when the mob was finally formed, the train had already passed carrying Chocano to freedom.

(Only three years later Chocano will return to Guatemala and give a recital in the Europa Theater. He will face a hostile public, anxious to take vengeance on the friend of the tyrant, but the poet's performance will be a triumphant display of both the power of his oratory and his poetry. Certainly, the dauntless spirit of Chocano looms clearly here.)

Nothing made Chocano deny his friendship and admiration for Estrada Cabrera. Indeed, his personal loyalty is equal to his boastfulness. "I never dissimulated nor denied this friendship, of which I feel very proud. . . . I was his friend long before I went to Mexico; I will continue being his friend, not only after he has fallen but even after he is dead."[19]

The poet spent several months in San José, Costa Rica, recuperating from the effects of prison life. It was then that he met the Aguilar Machado family. Toward the end of the year a war was threatening between Panama and Costa Rica. At long last Chocano decided to return to Peru.

VII   *Return to Peru: Triumph and Disgrace*

The poet arrived triumphantly in Lima on December 10, 1921, after an absence of almost seventeen years. Everywhere he was greeted with applause as Peru feted her renowned son. Chocano plunged into an immediate series of recitals given in all the principal cities of Peru, and each performance was an artistic and monetary success.

Augusto Leguía, who had interceded for the poet during his imprisonment in Guatemala, was then president of Peru, a ruler closely united to Chocano in political ideas. He was favorable to the plan of organizing a public recognition of Chocano as the nation's poet. Accordingly, the City Council of Lima headed the campaign for a national "Coronation," seconded by all the municipalities of the country. On November 5, 1922, the "Coronation" of the poet José Santos Chocano took place amid scenes of incredible adulation. All the cities of Peru were represented. The writers as a group, even those opposed to Chocano politically, paid him homage that day as poet. During the initial ceremony, held in the Palacio de la Exposición, President Leguía placed a circlet of gold laurel leaves upon Chocano's head. Uttering florid words of praise, the president called him "the most representative of the poets of America." Chocano replied: "Blessed are the countries who love their poets, for theirs is the kingdom of immortality. . . . Five million souls have been fused into one, which in glorifying my representative art glorifies also what my art represents. My art is made from history and nature; but . . . I have taken care not to contradict the Emersonian concept of the poet who, whether epic as Dante or lyric as Bryon, must sincerely harmonize his life with his art, until becoming the protagonist of his best poem. . . . The more one is of his Race and his Land, the more universally appreciated he will become; in Poets as in the trees, the thickest foliage corresponds to the deepest roots."[20] After the ceremonies at the Palace, a procession escorted the poet to the Plaza Bolognesi for the second part of these operatic scenes. Enormous crowds assembled for the speeches and music, and Chocano read the final part of his *La epopeya del Morro* beneath the monument to the hero of Arica. Amid wild clapping and shouting the procession formed again and made its way to the City Hall of Lima, where Chocano appeared on a balcony and spoke to the throngs below.

At the same time in another part of the city a bronze plaque was placed in the house where the "favorite son of the city of Lima" had been born. In the "Fiesta of Poets," held that evening in the Teatro Forero, the Poet Laureate of Peru listened to the extravagant eulogies in his honor, and he in turn recited many of his recent poems for this ecstatic audience.

The bitter episodes preceding Chocano's "Coronation" make the fervor in this ceremony even more remarkable. Unfortunately, Chocano was never able to concentrate solely on his poetry, and early in 1922 he had become embroiled in heated political debates. As a result he published a booklet entitled *Idearium tropical* (Tropical Ideas), a collection of various pieces having to do with his political views. His *Sumario del programa de la revolución mexicana* and his anti-imperialist speech given in Puerto Rico reappear here. But of more importance is a discussion praising dictatorships as opposed to the farce of a democracy: "Apuntes sobre las dictaduras organizadoras y la gran farsa demócrata" (Notes on Organizational Dictatorships and the Great Democratic Farce). Obviously this involved Chocano in his customary political turmoil, giving his enemies new weapons for claiming that he was an adulator of tyrants. In March, 1922, these political enemies sent the following telegram to a worldwide press: "Lima. The Peruvian poet José Santos Chocano, who was received upon his arrival with such enthusiastic acclaim by both the press and social and intellectual circles, even to the point of being called 'the favorite son of the city of Lima,' has fallen into disgrace because of the ideas that he has professed in this city concerning 'the necessity of tyrants in American Republics.'"[21] The powerful daily *El Comercio* reacted violently against Chocano. While one might not attack Leguía personally, his friend Chocano was a convenient target. In addition, these views hastened Chocano's estrangement from a certain sector of the Peruvian writers, principally those of the new generation who were restlessly groping toward literary expression of the problems of the vast indigenous majority in Peru.

There are ample reasons for believing, then, that Chocano's friends, led by Leguía, chose the "Coronation" as a means of vindicating Chocano publicly as well as honoring him as poet. The fact remains, however, that the writers did acclaim him fervently as a great poet, even those radically opposed to him in politics.

In the years 1923–24, Chocano traveled through Colombia, Venezuela, Panama, Costa Rica, El Salvador, and Guatemala, giving recitals. Everywhere there was admiration. These frequent trips gave the poet the opportunity to continue his courtship of Margarita Aguilar Machado, a courtship which had begun in secret in 1921, in San José, Costa Rica, where Chocano was recuperating from his prison ordeal. When Margarita's parents belatedly discovered the alliance, they were so incensed that it seemed prudent for Chocano to retreat. He returned to San José in February, 1924, with the necessary documents for their marriage, although Margarita had to elude her constant chaperones in order to meet the poet for the prearranged civil ceremony. Chocano was forty-nine and his bride little more than twenty-one. (This love inspired many lyric poems which Margarita published posthumously.)

The couple returned to Peru in April, 1924. Preparations were underway for the first centennial of the Battle of Ayacucho, to be held on December 9 of that year. President Leguía was anxious to celebrate it appropriately, and thus the government of Peru assigned Chocano to compose a great commemorative poem in honor of the date. The poet worked all the rest of the year on this task, projecting an immense epic work to be entitled *El Hombre-Sol* (The Sun-Man); he completed one long portion in verse, Canto IV: *Ayacucho y los Andes* (Ayacucho and the Andes), which was published in November. There is undeniable beauty in these lines, but there is also a glimmer of diminished power.

Other great American poets gathered for the centennial ceremonies, among them Leopoldo Lugones, Ricardo Jaimes Freyre, and Guillermo Valencia of the Modernist generation. At a recital given by these poets, Lugones declared: "For the good of the world the hour of the sword has arrived"[22] (referring to the rise of fascism in Italy). These words circulated in the presses of Latin America and were generally attributed to Chocano, since they were certainly similar to other pronouncements of his.

Chocano spent the months of February to June of 1925 in Venezuela, where he made financial arrangements for one thousand copies of his *Ayacucho y los Andes*. The tyrant Juan Vicente Gómez received him with special attention. Meanwhile a strong condemnation of "Chocano's words" had been published in a Mexican paper by the young Mexican writer and educator José Vasconcelos, who lamented that Chocano had left the lyre of the poet for the jingling rod of the buffoon. No one in Lima knew of this until the poet returned in June. Chocano persuaded his friend Clemente Palma, director of the daily *La Crónica*, to reproduce the article, and then he proceeded to answer the charges and to ridicule the author in extremely harsh terms. Vasconcelos had been elected "Youth's Teacher" by student groups in Peru, Colombia, and in other countries. The university students, therefore, became embroiled in the ensuing debate, particularly because Chocano represented the voice of Leguía, whose government had taken a definite turn toward dictatorship. Chocano reacted furiously against the Peruvian students, accusing them of ignorance and communism. The atmosphere was heated and overwrought. Fourteen intellectuals sought to intervene by pleading for a dispassionate spirit in the ideological discussions. Among these were Luis Alberto Sánchez, José Carlos Mariátegui, Edwin Elmore, Alcides Spelucín, Antenor Orrego, Eloy Espinosa, and John MacKay.

Edwin Elmore,[23] a young Peruvian writer, became especially involved through a hostile speech on station O.A.X. of Lima and in an article in which he denounced Chocano. By now the poet was in a frenzied mood, and he descended to the level of insulting the memory of Elmore's father, once tried for treason in the Battle of Arica against the Chileans but found not guilty. Chocano wrote: "Wretched young man: Although you are not to be blamed for having as a father a traitor to his country, I have the right to believe that the Chileans have paid you to insult me, as they paid your father to disclose the location of the mines that defended the Morro of Arica. . . . A Peruvian for whom a King, ten governments and three Congresses intervened, insulted by the son of the traitor of Arica! Scum! As I have smashed Vasconcelos, I will crush you, if you do not get on your knees to beg my pardon. For you I could not be other than your master."[24]

It is obvious that Chocano was beside himself with rage, even mixing the Spanish *tu* and *usted* forms of address in these wildly agitated lines. On the afternoon of the same day that he had written this vitriolic attack (October 31, 1925), he went to the offices of *El Comercio*. An angry Elmore had also gone to the same place to insert an open letter to Chocano. And there the two adversaries met.

Elmore was thirty-five; Chocano, fifty. Some accounts say that in an exchange of angry words, Elmore slapped Chocano in the face, and that then the poet stepped back, took out a pistol, and fired. Elmore staggered toward the door, wounded in the abdomen; his death came later during surgery.[25] Another version stresses that Elmore struck Chocano repeatedly, while Chocano tried to defend himself from the beating until he received a blow in the abdominal region. Then he took out his pistol and fired one shot at Elmore, who was able to reach the street but who died two days later as a consequence of surgical negligence.[26]

Chocano handed himself over to the authorities. This time he was not a political prisoner. In the city where three years before he had been crowned the National Poet of Peru, he was now imprisoned in the Hospital Militar de San Bartolomé.

The proceedings were rich with dramatic incidents. During his confinement in 1926 and part of 1927, Chocano published *La Hoguera*, an irregular weekly in which he attacked his opponents more than he defended himself. Never abandoning his olympic pride, he wrote verses full of blazing arrogance. "So many have slandered me/and have jeered at me/and have given such magnitude to my sin/that it grieves me not to have committed it."[27] A ringing sonnet entitled "La gloria del proceso" (The Glory of the Trial) begins with the lines: "Don Miguel de Cervantes will lend me his pen/to write my name beneath the lawsuit."[28]

He succeeded in having his wife, Margarita, accompany him in the Hospital Militar, and there his last son was born.

During his imprisonment Chocano prepared *El libro de mi proceso* (My Trial), which was published in Lima in 1927-28 in three volumes, and combined into one volume in Madrid in 1931. The work is interesting both as a psychological and as a literary document. In this book Chocano defends himself in great detail, and, in addition, revives all his public ideological disputes with the resultant abuse he has suffered. Many of his known and emotion-producing views are reiterated: "I have always preferred the dictatorship of one single responsible man ... to that of a few wealthy families who irresponsibly divide among themselves the life of the Republic."[29] Such statements are incredible to a North American, since neither alternative makes sense; but to a Peruvian, especially of that day, these were the only choices.

What Chocano's friends and enemies expected him to do was to rest his defense upon the fact that a younger man had slapped him in the face and that he had reacted in anger, which he regretted. The proud Chocano could not stoop to this. He preferred to state that he considered himself innocent and that the true cause of death was due to the error of the surgeon (Dr. Guillermo Gastañeta, dean of the School of Medicine of San Marcos, and a relative of Elmore). He also made an effort to present himself as a kind of avenger of an offended country by characterizing Elmore as the son of a traitor to Peru. In spite of the torments and the hatred that surrounded him, Chocano maintained his proud personality and aplomb. And in accord with his previous character he saw fit to attack not only Dr. Gastañeta, but the oligarchy that he had always scorned, ·this time in the person of Antonio Miró Quesada, owner and publisher of *El Comercio*, whose testimony of the encounter with Elmore was hostile.

Because of the fame of Chocano, the case had the engrossed attention of the nation. It must be remembered that Peru is a small country and thus, somewhat like the saga of a family, every event is interrelated with another. For example, although Elmore's father had been declared not guilty of treason, and although this fact of forty-five years past had nothing to do with the case, feelings engendered by the war with Chile still ran high, and there was a whole generation in sympathy with Chocano's ideas. This group believed that he had been insulted unjustly by a younger man and had therefore been provoked to defend his honor. The younger generation, especially the intellectuals who had already been alienated from the poet, reacted against "Leguía's friend," whom they considered a common murderer. They bitterly deplored the heaping of abuse upon the victim by attaching the stigma of treason to his family name.

On June 22, 1926, Chocano was declared guilty. He was condemned to three years in prison—until October 31, 1928—and was fined two thousand pounds (Peruvian) to be paid to Elmore's widow. Peruvian and Latin American intellectuals immediately organized a vast campaign to obtain the poet's freedom. Although Elmore had become a symbol of opposition to dictatorship and abuse of power, the figure of Chocano, the poet, still produced deep sentiments, especially among the best-known writers of Latin America. They signed a petition asking for his pardon. Chocano was adamant. In a letter to his lawyer he stated that he would never accept a pardon, because while this might excuse the penalty it would also accept the existence of the crime, which he would not admit.

Finally the Congress of Peru approved a law of amnesty, conforming to the Constitution and the Penal Code of the Republic. The crime was put aside, and Chocano was freed on December 10, 1927.

In the first days of his freedom the poet walked arrogantly through the streets of Lima, not wishing to reveal how alone he felt, nor how deeply affected by past events. This attitude increased his isolation even more. By May he had decided to live in Chile, but he delayed his departure month after month. At last in November he left Lima—city of his greatest triumph and his most tragic hours.

VIII   *Last Years in Chile*

Many times Chocano had spoken against the conquerors of the War of the Pacific, but the Chileans received him with sheltering hospitality. He went to Santiago, and there he lived the remainder of his life with Margarita and their son, Jorge Santos.

The newspapers wrote glowingly about him. At that time Peru and Chile were recementing their friendship, interrupted some sixty years ago. In addition, Chocano had written a pamphlet on "How the Plebiscite of Tacna and Arica Should be Carried Out," which had been published in the presses of both Lima and Santiago in July, 1925, soon after the Arbitration Award issued by President Coolidge. After a detailed explanation of procedures, Chocano had written: "My country's enemy will not find hatred wrapped up in my words. . . . There is no hatred for anyone, but love for justice in the name of continental interests."[30]

It is obvious that Chocano tried earnestly to rebuild his life. In the turmoil that had followed the fall of Estrada Cabrera in Guatemala, he had lost a great number of poems. Now in Santiago he began new work; and he put in order the poetry of past years. He collaborated in the local *El Mercurio* and *La Nación*, and he sent material to *La Nación* and *La Prensa* of Buenos Aires. Every day he was seen in the midst of the business district. The necessity of sustaining himself and his family was obvious, but his inextinguishable pride accompanied him in his poverty.

This was the time in which he looked back upon the drama of his life, filled with vivid memories. He intended to publish his *Memorias* in book form, but economically it was advantageous to have them appear simultaneously, 1930–31, in several newspapers of the Continent (including *La Noche* of Lima). The *Memorias* stop around the year 1907. Whether they were to be finished or whether the 1908 events in Spain were too traumatic to write down is not certain.

In 1931, the poet's mother died in Lima, but her son was unable to pay for the trip to Peru. The story circulated that he had to pawn his poet's crown in order to cover his immediate expenses.[31]

At the end of 1932, a conflict broke out between Peru and Colombia. Chocano, who had always been an ardent supporter of continentalism, published a pamphlet entitled *El escándalo de Leticia* (The Scandal of Leticia)—the name of the territorial zone in dispute—in which he attacked the strangling rule of the Peruvian tyrant Luis Sánchez Cerro. There were large groups of Peruvian intellectuals, politicians, and students in Chile at that time, most of them in exile for opposition to the outrages of Sánchez Cerro. Yet while they were in agreement with Chocano on this point, they were not in accord with the former regime of Leguía. Hence, Chocano had few friendly contacts with his countrymen in exile, and for the most part the Peruvians in Chile left him alone. Some of his letters from that period reveal the hostile environment that enveloped him but which pride would not allow him to admit. These same letters show the tenacity with which he fought the reverses of fortune, his confidence in old friends, and his hope of retaking his position of former times.

Much of the poetry written during this closing period of his life is shorn of oratorical emphasis and glorifying personal or continental pomp. Two beautiful poems allow a glimpse of a chastened soul: "Elegía hogareña" (Elegy to a Home, 1931 or 1932), in memory of his mother; and "Finigénito" (The Lastborn, 1934), for his seven-year-old son, to whom he puts the question, "Will not the weight of my name break your angel wings?"[32] The sweet sadness cast over the lines of these two compositions reveals the state of Chocano's spirit, now in the last years of his fifties.

He wrote incessantly during those years. He gathered his poems, revised and carefully edited, for the volumes of *Oro de Indias* (The Gold of the Indies). In the midst of his dire financial problems, he decided to publish *Primicias de oro de Indias* (First Fruits from the Gold of the Indies) in 1934, which he circulated as a kind of advance sampling of the coming *Oro de Indias*. The book revived much of Chocano's past literary reputation and was hailed by many critics (outside Peru).

Again there was a public ceremony honoring Chocano as poet, this time at the National University of Chile. The poetess Juana de Ibarbourou of Uruguay gave the address of homage in the name of the poets of America. When Chocano rose to respond to the plaudits in his honor, a voice from the crowd yelled, "Murderer. Elmore's murderer." Chocano stopped his own words and answered, "Cowards cling to the darkness. If you are a man stand out in the open." The rector of the university hastened to his feet and stated with conviction, "Distinguished poet, that was neither a Chilean nor a Peruvian. Neither country would be proud of such a man." The ceremony continued with no further interruptions.[33]

As he was continuously plagued by the lack of money, Chocano had become obsessed with projects of finding a supposedly hidden treasure of the Jesuits. Ultimately this led to his death, in a form as dramatic as his whole life had been.

On the afternoon of December 13, 1934, Chocano mailed two letters to friends in Montevideo concerning arrangements for recitals there in April. Always superstitious, he dated them December 14 to avoid the number 13, although both were post-marked the 13th. He got on a streetcar and sat down near the back on one of the lateral seats near the ticket collector. Minutes before five o'clock, a tall, thin man got on the streetcar and stood near the front. He stared at someone behind him and then began to back up through the aisle until he was next to Chocano. Suddenly he lunged at the poet, and with two swift movements the assailant stabbed his victim twice in the chest, and with renewed fury he repeated the thrusts in his back. Chocano collapsed, spilling torrents of blood in the midst of the frightened passengers. The streetcar stopped and the police hastened to the scene. Chocano was taken immediately to the nearest hospital, and on the way he gasped, "Hurry, please. My heart hurts so." By the time they reached the hospital, the poet was dead.[34] Many years before (*Alma América*, 1906) Chocano had written these prophetic lines to close his sonnet "La muerte de Pizarro" (The Death of Pizarro): "He who took a life by assault/ could only die by a sword thrust."

The assassin, Manuel Bruce Badilla, made no protest when they took him prisoner. Apparently he believed that Chocano was depriving him of treasure which was rightfully his.[35] He was later declared insane and was put into an asylum.

Chocano's widow and their young son were left in absolute poverty. The Chilean government paid for an impressive funeral, and the Barzelatto family of Santiago lent a mausoleum for the body. Not even his burial place was his own!

Many of Chocano's books were published posthumously, principally from the work he had prepared and collected during his years in Chile: *Poemas del amor doliente* (Poems of a Suffering Love, 1937); *Oro de Indias*, Volumes I and II (1939, 1940) and Volumes III and IV (1941); *Memorias. Las mil y una aventuras* (1940); *El alma de Voltaire y otras prosas* (The Soul of Voltaire and Other Prose, 1940). Anthologies were edited in Paris, Montevideo, and Bogotá.

In *Iras santas* a young poet had defiantly stated: "Oh ungrateful country, you do not deserve to have my remains."[36] In 1945, a group of deputies presented a bill to the Peruvian Congress which proposed that Chocano's body be brought back to Peru at the government's expense. No one protested, but somehow successive governments never got around to fulfilling the law.

Thirty-one years after his death, when feelings about Chocano the man had subsided in favor of Chocano the poet, the Peruvian government finally honored her native son. On May 14, 1965, precisely the date of his birth ninety years before, Chocano's body was flown from Santiago to Lima. Accorded the honors of minister of state, his casket was covered by the Peruvian flag. After a brief ceremony at the airport, the entourage moved to the University of San Marcos where the dean of the Faculty of Letters, Dr. Augusto Tamayo Vargas, spoke in honor of the poet. On the following day a solemn funeral procession formed to accompany the body to Presbítero Maestro Cemetery. The procession included members of the clergy, state dignitaries, government troops, and members of Chocano's family, among the latter his third wife, Margarita, their son Jorge Santos (the "lastborn," then nearing forty), two older children by his second wife, and six grandchildren. At the graveside there were speeches and poetry. Juan Guzmán Cruchaga, Chilean poet who had accompanied the body as ambassador extraordinary from his country, spoke these words: "José

Santos Chocano, there is no proud and superb voice like the one which burned in your throat."[37] According to Chocano's own desires, he was buried in an upright position,[38] in a burial plot of one square yard on the surface. José Santos Chocano was at last on Peruvian soil.

The life of Chocano is difficult to put into focus. One who has left behind such a legendary trail of adventures becomes somehow more a legendary figure than an actual person. In his lifetime Chocano's name brought forth too fervent praise and too prejudiced condemnation. The same oversized emotions have followed him in the critiques, especially in the years immediately following his death, when analysis of his poetry was often overshadowed by commentaries of his life.

Certain aspects of Chocano the man are abundantly clear. The haughty poet of Lima was aristocratic by nature, and his pride, innate and habitual. He himself says: "In art as in life, I have always tried to be the master of my own personality. . . . I believe that I have never become confused with others, not even with those whom I have esteemed as equal to me."[39] This pride led to contemptuous arrogance when it came up against personally unfavorable situations, but it also fed the springs of his indomitable spirit in adversity. This poet never ceased to be Chocano, even in his most tormented moments.

His personal amorality is certainly one facet of his artistic temperament, and it is obvious that Chocano considered himself above and superior to ordinary laws. He, better than anyone else, has synthesized his esthetic and worldly conduct in line after line of his poetry.

He was pompous, magnificently arrogant, peremptory, decisive, and charming. He was solemn and majestic in his gestures, and disarming in his sudden impulses. He was polished, superstitious, often ostentatious, and he lacked a sense of humor. All these attitudes appear in his poetry.

We can picture him in any political situation, but always in rebellion. He was often inspired and genuinely affected by emotions. If he was a Catholic in his boyhood, his Catholicism became little more than ornamental. He liked to consider himself a Don Juan—and his amorous deeds proclaim the success of this pose—yet his love poetry possesses few lines of tenderness with the exception of one posthumous book. Only in front of his mother did he put aside pretense, and indeed she is the source of some of his imperishable poetry. His letters to her throughout his incessant journeys show the sincere concern of a dutiful son. He also accepted full financial responsibility for all his children.

Chocano exhibited an undaunted zest for life and a penchant for living in the storm eye of turmoil. He was a man who seethed with driving ambitions, and yet he was ingenuous and full of candor. He said he had no childhood, but often he seemed a man who never matured.

Perhaps his own lines, which he dedicated to Pancho Villa, are most apt to describe him: "A demon and an angel, in tremendous strife, disputed your destiny. . . Therefore when you are alone, unwillingly you feel the beating of four wings within your heart."[40]

Chocano's tempestuous life is particularly difficult for the North American to assess; yet all his poetry stems precisely from this life, as he himself said many times: "I always compose my verse after I have lived it."[41] The Peruvian writer Luis Alberto Sánchez offers astute advice for a complete understanding of the man and his work: "We must put ourselves into Chocano's times and not try to focus his finisecular and sometimes crowd-pleasing poetry with today's neon lights and sophistication."[42]

Chocano's effortless poetry welled up from his restless and dramatic life. Yet beneath the flamboyant exterior there also lies a resume of the disoriented Peruvian artist of his epoch, an epoch which spans the last years of the nineteenth century and more than a quarter of this century.

CHAPTER 2

The Youthful Poet

THE balance between the rhythm of Chocano's life and his surging poetry can be seen from the beginning of his work. The first period of creativity covers some ten years, from age eighteen to around twenty-eight, a time in which Chocano evolved from a groping poet into an established artist. The style ripens, slowly but perceptively; at the end of this period it has taken definite form.

I   *Repudiated Verses of Early Adolescence*

Through silence Chocano disclaimed the verses of his early adolescence. None of his first books mention them, not even his *Poesías completas* (1902). Unlike Darío, who rewrote but never repudiated his adolescent work, Chocano's reticence clearly shows the opinion he held of these early poems. It is curious that the poet, so mindful of his image, did not destroy them, for they are in fact of little substance and promise. The verses have come to public attention only because Chocano's oldest son published them in a posthumous volume called *Páginas de oro de José Santos Chocano* (Golden Pages from José Santos Chocano) in which the original handwritten copies are reproduced, including corrections, crossed out passages, and a frequent "*No!*"

The collection in *Páginas* begins with verses which his son says were written before the poet was ten years old. The few poems which are dated give the years 1890 and 1891, when Chocano was fifteen and sixteen, and possibly one or two verses belong to 1892. Occasionally the poet uses a pseudonym, "Bíbolo," beside his own name. From both the form and the content it is apparent that the young Chocano was an avid reader of the Spanish Post-Romantic poet, Gustavo Adolfo Bécquer. The influence of other writers can also be identified, particularly Salvador Díaz Mirón and Manuel González Prada from Latin America, and Victor Hugo and Ramón de

Campoamor from Europe. The material is of varied meter and theme, with numerous sonnets dedicated to his mother, to Victor Hugo, Clemente Palma, González Prada, and several compositions in honor of Peru and her heroes. There is music and dissonance, lament and protest, and the sentiments typical of his age—all enveloped in high sounding phrases. Actually there are few indications of the imaginative figures and flashing metaphors so characteristic of Chocanesque poetry. Thus, respecting the opinion of Chocano himself, we will turn to what he considered his first works.

II   *Poetry of 1895–96*

Chocano's first two books of poetry reflect two dominant facets in the poet's spirit: rebellion and an absorbing love of nature. These will develop simultaneously into the mature epic-lyric poet, still inspired by the same vibrant emotions.

The extravagant Peruvian popularity of Chocano began with his *Iras santas: poesías americanas* (1895). The author was twenty and had just faced death for defying the tyrant Cáceres. A wave of adulation swept over the country. Peru had been brought to her knees by the War of the Pacific and had existed in chaos and spiritual stagnation since that time. Suddenly this youthful shout of defiance, full of unabashed pride—pride in self, pride in being a Peruvian—helped to rekindle the feelings of national pride so crushed by the Chilean defeat. Indeed this gallant ability to lift his head and face adversity is a major note in the poet's life and poetry. The civil revolution headed by Piérola had triumphed, and Chocano, who had suffered dramatic imprisonment for this cause, was part of the triumph.

Printed in red ink, *Iras santas* trembles with the rage of passionate youth. The unhappy circumstances of his country call for battle and the young poet hastens to the combat. "Oh poets! The clash of swords calls us/Struggle and toil call to us."[1] Of fiery nature, Chocano is little given to brooding. Virile aggressiveness is the poet's answer. "Today that sad country, crouched in a corner, must become inflamed. . . . Ruins belong to oblivion: let us remake the destroyed, let us lift again the fallen."[2]

At twenty Chocano already has a messianic concept of his mission and his destiny. He is the arrogant spirit who will shatter the yoke and bring redemption: "The poet is a redeemer who sings;

therefore, he should say to Lazarus: Arise! and to Justice: Return to life!"[3] Without hesitation Chocano states: "If it is necessary for another Christ to die, I am here."[4]

These heroic expressions are part of the hyperbole, of the bombast in the entire work, which are perhaps excusable in the brashness of youth and especially in the light of Peru's turmoil at that time. *Iras santas* blazes with the indignation of a very young man in the face of social injustice and tyranny, and the bellicose verses rage in capital letters and end in exclamation points.

A curious mixture of anarchism and patriotic fervor runs through the pages. This is a defiant singer, an enemy of the existing society, and in his zeal to destroy the present regime, Chocano appears to be an advocate of an idealistic system. Grandly he demands universal equality: "If all are equal in death/let all be equal in life."[5] In his "El sermón de la montaña," dedicated to Rubén Darío, he has no compunction about blending his own words with those of Christ. Indeed, the divine figure of the Gospels merges into the spirit of the poet, proclaiming a rebel doctrine of social principles: "In this world you have as equal a right to receive the sun on your foreheads as to receive God in your heart." In spite of the magnetic mass appeal of these verses, especially at that difficult time in Peru, the reader of Chocano knows full well that the idea of equality could never find a permanent place in this arrogant and individualistic poet.

The ten poems of "En la mazmorra" (In the Dungeon) are the most moving, particularly because of the circumstances in which they were written. The poet says of liberty: "She has been the light of my twenty years:/God has given her to me and man has taken her away." In an ever increasing facility of metaphor Chocano sings his defiance of tyranny, until the final, proud taunt to his perverse enemies: "I will bury them in the prison of my verses; and my lyre will be their prison bars."

After his imprisonment he wrote "Juicio final" (The Last Judgment), which can be called a summary of the political situation in Peru, but applicable to any Spanish American revolution. Chocano rejoices in his triumphant release, reflects on his unjust betrayal, and then hurls insults at the fallen tyrant—the one who dreamed of greatness but instead revealed his emptiness and smallness (small even in his vices), thus reaping the final disdainful judgment of his victims, his country, and history.

Chocano's guides throughout these verses were Díaz Mirón, Espronceda, and Hugo. Particularly similar is the tone of blazing indignation and personal pride struck by both the Mexican Díaz Mirón in his early poetry and the Peruvian Chocano here and in later works.

There is a surge of crowd-pleasing excitement, of dramatic popular appeal in these declamatory verses. Yet the small group which made up the cultured elite was also pleased with the work because of Chocano's effortless use of technical forms still comparatively new and untried in Peru. "It is usually granted that this work, together with two more from the same years, ushered in Peruvian Modernism. Bursting upon the Peruvian scene with a resounding din, Chocano was soon at the head of the Modernist movement in Peru, surrounded by innumerable admirers and imitators. Adulated and adored, Chocano for some time filled the small world of Peruvian letters."[6] (Chocano's place in continental Modernism will be discussed in Chapter 4.)

En la aldea: poesías americanas (1895) should be approached as a compensation for the bursting restlessness of *Iras santas*. This is the beginning of Chocano's devotion to nature, a hint of what will be the core of his later poetry. *En la aldea* reflects the peace of a Peruvian village, actually a bouquet of impressions from many little towns, with Chorrillos as the centerpiece. The fragrance of the countryside is here, the nights by the sea, the joyful summer mornings. Nature is dressed in soft colors, and her face is calm. She is seen in the wheat from which comes the Host, in the spray of the surf reaching up to Heaven, in the soul of each flower. With simplicity the poet paints the religious processions, the fishermen with their nets and oars, the stooped schoolmaster. The titles of the poems announce the dominant spirit: "The Prayer," "The Stream," "The Sunset," "The Plow Horse," "Old Trees."

The sea is an inspiration for a young man living within constant sight and sound of the Pacific. Gazing at the pounding waves, the youthful poet composed the sonnet "Playera" (Breaking Surf), so different in tone from the arrogant and unyielding Chocano.

Playera

Filósofo es el mar: se alza y se llena
y después de estallar en broncos ruidos,
corta su voz, apaga sus latidos,
y se dilata en la extensión serena.

Sabe que hay una ley que lo refrena;
y sus sueños al ver desvanecidos,
se queja con furiosos alaridos
y como un gladiador rueda en la arena.

Almas que el ansia de luchar obstina:
venid conmigo a la arenosa raya
y veréis cómo el mar también se inclina;

que el rendirse ¡ay! cuando el vigor se abruma,
es solamente respetar la playa,
y dejar de ser ola, y ser espuma.

Breaking Surf

Philosophic is the sea: it rises fully,
and after bursting into raucous sobs,
quells its voice, extinguishes its throbs,
and spreads into expanses of serenity.

It feels itself restrained by law of unseen hand;
and when its dreams disintegrate, in vain
cries out with furious shrieks of pain
and like a gladiator rolls upon the sand.

Oh souls where yearnings for great combat flow,
come with me to the sandy line
and watch how the sea must also bend low.

For to submit when greater forces scoff
is but to respect the shoreline,
and to cease being a wave, to become sea froth.

P. R-P.

En la aldea was printed in blue ink, and the color was not only a contrast to the red of *Iras santas* but of special meaning in Modernism. Darío's *Azul* . . . (Azure) had appeared in 1888, and making a slight reverence in the direction of the master, Chocano's work has a "Preludio azul" (Blue Prelude). Here the poet asks that his verses be devoured, all their sap extracted, for the greatest of his pleasures is to see them die like the petals of the flowers which women idly tear off one by one.

Although Chocano published *Iras santas* earlier in the same year and immediately became the accepted leader of Peruvian Modernism, *En la aldea* possesses many more obvious Modernist notes.

A white swan arches its neck in the waters of a lagoon, where a willow sheds tears of faded leaves. "La nota gris" (The Gray Note) pays homage to the synthesis of color and image in the Modernist scheme (although instead of the emphasis of other Modernist color pieces, Chocano's echoes a tone of hope and final resurrection). The picaresque and malicious irony of the *limeño* (native of Lima) is expressed in the sonnet "El Buey" (The Ox). Among the lasting poems in this vein is "En la alcoba" (In the Love Nest), full of eroticism, grace, and irony.

Chocano's undisputed position as the leader in Peruvian Modernism rested in great part upon his use of the new poetic forms. He displays an extensive repertoire within the intricate patterns of Spanish versification and gracefully employs many known but rarely used meters. The parade of metrical skills which files by in the poetry of *En la aldea* is all the more interesting when we recall that Darío's *Prosas profanas* (Secular Prose), considered the highest point in the development of Modernist poetry, was published one year later.

More than the other works of this first period, *En la aldea* presages the consummate artist of *Alma América*, eleven years in the future. Here is the young painter of birds, snakes, landscapes, of American fauna and flora. Here the literary figures seem a rehearsal for the symphony of *Alma América*. The toad is "a stone with life"; "the wind sweeps the dry leaves from the ground with its enormous wing"; "the trees—soldiers of guerrilla warfare—guard the dusty road"; "the stars appear like acolytes."[7]

Chocano endows the things of nature with a life of their own, a kind of animistic tendency he never completely abandoned. Thus in "En la campiña" (In the Countryside) the proud trees stand on tiptoe; the sun, like an executioner, chastises the fields; the peaks of the mountains exhibit their splendor; the plow goes to the furrow; the creek laughs and whispers.

Yet not all is peace. In 1881, Chorrillos had been burned by the Chilean troops, and when Chocano wrote these poems, probably in the summer and fall of 1893, there was still evidence of the destruction caused by the war. Therefore the rebellious Chocano is prompted to insert among his youthful watercolors several violent denunciations, reminiscent of the caustic phrases in *Iras santas:* "Oh sad victim of stupid warfare, who lies sleeping,/Oh ruined village, resting your head in barren dust!"[8] "La Invasión" (The Invasion),

"El Cementerio" (The Cemetery), "En el tren" (On the Train), "Aquí estoy" (I Am Here), "Ultratumba," (Beyond the Tomb), and others, all contain his anger.

The subtitle of both *Iras santas* and *En la aldea: poesías americanas* (American Poetry) reveals that even at this early stage (1893–95), Chocano possessed the incipient plan to be the voice of popular continental beauty as well as the voice of popular continental desires.

Manuel González Prada said of *Iras santas* that Chocano seized poetry by the hair and shook her severely.[9] Correspondingly he should have added that the poet smoothed her tresses back tenderly in *En la aldea*. The two works of 1895 balance and complement each other. In *Iras santas* rebellion and protest are uppermost, with Chocano himself as the hero of the epic. Perhaps only one poem, "La Alondra" (The Lark), represents the softer side. It is uneven, torrential, and bombastic, but it possesses a certain exuberant freshness. *En la aldea* is lyric for the most part, with tentative steps in the direction of Modernism and a sprinkling of the fiery defiance always present in the poet's character. In these two works the seed was planted which was to grow into the forked maturity of an epic-lyric poet.

Azahares (1896) completes the trilogy of these early years. This collection of twelve poems, inspired by Chocano's coming marriage to Consuelo Bermúdez, quite naturally falls on the lyric side of the poet's work. Actually the volume contributed little to Chocano's poetic reputation.

Throughout this love poetry there is a striving for effect, and an uncomfortable sensation persists that Chocano is purposely striking the expected pose of an ardent lover. His wish to impress Consuelo with his role of virile and aggressive male leads to such exaggerated lines as: "The formidable lion, whose roar brings horror, retracts his sharp claws when he courts the lioness."[10] Chocano never loses sight of himself as triumphant hero and radiant poet. The metaphors and similes do not approach those of his first two books; indeed when Chocano states "I opened my book, like God His heavens/and I saw my verses, like God His worlds,"[11] it must be admitted that the imagery has gone astray.

Chocano himself expressed his opinion of *Azahares* by excluding it from *¡Fiat Lux!*, the definitive anthology of his youthful work.

III   *Poetry to 1901*

The poetry of these early years continued to flow without inter-
ruption, exhibiting Chocano's efforts toward poetic growth. In this
context *Selva virgen: poemas y poesías* (1898?)[12] is a transition piece
in which the poet experiments with many styles and influences.

The title can be traced to the deep impressions of his trip to the
Peruvian jungles around 1896, although the emotion generated
from that first contact with the interior of Peru shines later in
El Derrumbe rather than in this work. (And in spite of the title,
there was more concern with nature in the earlier *En la aldea* than
in this collection.)

The title page bears two mottoes, thus beginning the characteristic *imprimatur* which will accompany most books by Chocano.
From the Latin phrase "With this sign you will conquer" it is
obvious that Chocano means he will conquer by his lyre rather than
by the cross. The Spanish motto—"In my art all models fit as in
a ray of light all the colors of the spectrum"—is a clear announce-
ment that he is not bound by strict adherence to any school,
including Modernism, the dominant influence of that epoch. This
motto, or a variation, will preface his best works.

A few of the poems in *Selva virgen* show some pictorial aspects
of the nature he viewed, but more as trappings than anything else.
Actually in this collection the work drawn from nature results in
some of the most absurd imagery. The opening poem "La voz de la
selva" (The Voice of the Forest) brings a mixture of description: the
footfall of the beast, the laughter of the river, the complaint of a
falling leaf; a pagan muse pursued by a savage with painted
feathers. Uniting these diverse figures the poet adds: "May the
fleeing muse leave her sweet name, written in Greek letters, on a
trunk of this American forest." In the closing poem, "El amor de
las selvas" (Love in the Jungles), Chocano uses figures from the
selva to give a startling effect to a love poem. He wishes he were a
boa so he could die squeezing his lady's beauty, or a jaguar in order
to tear open his love and see if she possesses a heart!

Other poems reach a higher level of artistry. Aiming at intense
and emotional poetry, Chocano creates three lasting compositions:
the poignantly sad "Urna" (Urn), in memory of a little child;
"El último amor" (The Last Love), a sensitive portrayal by a young
poet praising the provocative beauty of an autumnal love; and

"De viaje" (Traveling), an expressive description of a passing encounter: "Perhaps we will never meet again. Perhaps we will propel the same ship of love, she on one side and I on the other, like two oars, all our lives rowing together and separated all our lives". The sweet melancholy of the latter, an insistent minor chord heard throughout Chocano's work, is much more moving as love poetry than his studied ardor. The opening phrase, "Ave de paso" (Bird in flight), became reality for the poet, initiator of so many loves which were never fulfilled because of his erratic life.

Chocano's earliest poetry was often injured by his uncontrolled emotion. In contrast *Selva virgen* possesses a few sonnets that have been finely wrought, such as "Arqueología" (Archeology). It has been said that this composition is an example of the objectivity for which Chocano was striving. Particularly striking is the final rapier thrust.

Arqueología

Cuando en las viejas ruinas del Oriente
moderno explorador halla un tesoro,
al descubrir los ídolos de oro
que culto fueron de pagana gente,

¡con qué interés el alma del Presente
vuela a esa Edad, en que el sagrado coro
divinizaba en cántico sonoro
deformes monstruos de achatada frente!

Mañana que esta Edad también sucumba,
futuro explorador, de tumba en tumba,
paseará por las ruinas su mirada:

¡Y qué espanto tendrá, qué rara idea,
cuando brillar entre las ruinas vea,
como joya rarísima, una espada!

Archeology

Searching mid Eastern ruins, groping slow,
When some explorer in our modern days
His hand upon a hidden treasure lays—
Gold idols heathens worshipped long ago—
Then with what eager interest aglow
The spirit of the Present backward strays
To that far age when priests raised hymns of praise
To monstrous gods deformed, with foreheads low!

When our age too is dead, from tomb to tomb
Some new explorer, groping in the gloom,
Will search for what the ruins may afford.
How great his fear, how strange his thoughts will be
When, gleaming mid the shadows, he shall see,
Rarest, most precious treasure trove, a sword!

translation by Alice Stone Blackwell

In *Selva virgen* Chocano roams through various styles, illustrating, in different stages of development, all the facets of his art that we have seen so far. There are visible traces of Zorrilla: "Fin de don Juan" (The End of Don Juan); and themes favored by Echegaray: "El diálogo de las tumbas" (Dialogue of the Tombs). There is the sting of an ironic retort, gracefully phrased in the accepted *limeña* manner: "Punto final" (Closing Point). There is the dualism of "La vejez virgiliana" (Virgilian Old Age) and "La vejez anacreóntica" (Anacreontic Old Age).

Some of the poetry takes on the definite hues of Modernism. The delicate watercolor "Asunto Watteau" (Watteau Affair), replete with princess, fragrant gardens, and shepherds, is worthy of the title. "Pagana" (The Pagan), a hymn to the perfection of a statue, falls clearly in the center of Modernism, particularly in the final stanza where an unclothed nymph runs through the forest. (The poet's shadow will serve to cover her.) The swan often appears and there is an ample sprinkling of neo-Hellenist and neo-Roman references.

The poet does not make too much effort to display technical virtuosity, with the exception of "El nuevo dodecasílabo" (The New Twelve-Syllable Line), dedicated to Amado Nervo. "El verso futuro" (Future Verse), written in free verse, is dedicated to the Modernists Leopoldo Lugones and Ricardo Jaimes Freyre. Greatly exaggerated for the most part, it appears to welcome this style for the new liberty it gives the artist (although it might have been intended as satire if this were Chocano's strong point). "Why artifice if the spontaneous is beautiful? . . . Oh make free verse, resume of aesthetic triumphs, a sign of the art of the Americas."

A discussion of range in style and subject does not imply that the impetuous Chocano has cast off his protests nor his glorifying self-assertions. "Heroismo," with the flavor of his past violence, is a summons to the poets to enter into the strife. In "Imprecación" he states that he cannot descend to the level of others, that although his songs may inspire, he must view the smallness of humanity from above. In "Aguilas y gorriones" (Eagles and Sparrows) he writes that sparrows need to band together to cross the sky, but eagles fly alone. It is clear to all that Chocano sees himself as an eagle! His sonnet "Protesta," directed at his enemies, is indicative of many pieces which will come from a pen that finds it necessary to proclaim defiance of criticism. Much more arrogant is "Canto de huelga" (A Protest Song) in which the poet addresses the crowd: "Inane masses. If you are a river my soul is an ocean into which a thousand souls can empty." Chocano always considered himself vastly superior to the crowd, and yet we know that he fed on its applause.

Selva virgen is still hesitant, but is oriented now toward a defined path. The poet aspires to represent a country and an epoch, in a manner different from others. He does not attain his goals, but he has set about attaining them. There is evidence of his growing facility, especially in the direction of dazzling metaphors. If *Azahares* stood still (rather than to say that it was a step backward), *Selva virgen* takes a long stride toward the poetic ascendancy of *Alma América*.

Moving rapidly toward greater artistry, Chocano had two poetic triumphs in 1899, each of which enhanced his literary reputation in Peru and in Latin America: *La epopeya del Morro: poema americano* and *El Derrumbe: poema americano*. Again, as in the two works of 1895, these illustrate the dual nature of his poetry; one is a powerful epic work, the other is intensely lyrical. In the epic content of *La epopeya del Morro* Chocano discovered one path to fame; the magnificent, powerful nature seen in *El Derrumbe* provided another. Both converged into the beckoning highway leading to the coveted title of "Poet of America."

La epopeya del Morro celebrates the fervent patriotism and heroism of the Peruvian cavalry troops fighting against the invading Chileans during the Battle of Arica. Referring to historically accurate events of June 7, 1880, the episode throbs with deeds and names that are a source of great pride to Peruvians. A small band of men, under the command of Colonel Francisco Bolognesi, is defending the *Morro* (cliff) of the port of Arica. They wait in vain for reinforcements and face sad disillusion when what seems to be help proves instead to be the enemy. A messenger is

sent from the Chilean forces to offer the Peruvians their lives if
they will surrender. Vastly outnumbered and surrounded, defeat is
certain; yet the hero, Bolognesi, chooses to fight "to the last
cartridge" rather than surrender. Before giving his final rejection
he calls in his officers, who concur in his heroic attitude. The attack
begins. "Five times greater, the enemy will sweep away everything,
everything. It does not matter. Five times greater will be the
renown that each hero will take with him to the tomb."[13] A
woman dies on the battlefield, unwilling to leave her beloved's
side, and she becomes the symbol of the fallen *Patria*. Bolognesi,
mounted on his black charger, slashes at his enemies, fighting
desperately against all odds. But Death arrives, and like an arrow
her gaze pierces the hero. There is the dull thud of a body slipping
to earth, and the trot of a frightened, riderless horse. Another
Peruvian hero, Alfonso Ugarte, seeing himself surrounded by
the enemy, turns his horse around and in a great leap from the
cliff plunges into the sea, preferring death to capture. The first
night of captivity falls over the *Morro*. In a splendid climax
Chocano proclaims that the wounded Country must make a funeral pyre of branches cut from its tree of life, and as an offering
to its dead heroes must throw on it past vices, outmoded laws,
and sordid customs. When the past is consumed by the fire, the
future will rise from the ashes, and the nation's banner will float
over the ruins "like a sudden blaze become a flag."[14]

The robust, epic breath of *La epopeya del Morro* is combined with
excellent imagery: "Thus Death, in her savage fury, unwillingly
will feel the rejoicing of the traveler who arrives after a long
journey and falls into the arms of her children;" "The starving
troops, still erect, do not implore alms from Luck; they are like an
advance guard of Life presenting arms to Death"; "Life is only a
group of years that fights against an unknown Eternity"; "The
wave, sorrowfully kissing him, wrapped him in the winding sheet
of her spray"; "The Morro . . . is like a catafalque that exhibits the
body of an embalmed country."[15]

Written in the same vein of rebellion as some of his earlier
works, *La epopeya del Morro* displays a firmer touch, and in its
final form of 1908, a much more disciplined approach. It is certainly
more palatable to have the poet apply his vehement fervor to an
epic poem which glorifies Peruvian heroes than to self-glorification,
regardless of the circumstances.

It is evident that the poetic outbursts of patriotism by González Prada have influenced Chocano, although the manner of expression is quite different. As in other works, Chocano mingles Biblical and classical references. He can still be accused of wandering now and then into excessive wordiness or an occasional exaggerated statement (for example, using three Homeric heroes to characterize one Peruvian: "The great Bolognesi was the synthesis of Agamemnon, Nestor, and Achilles").[16] But as a whole the action moves swiftly, the poem flames with emotion, and while the lightning metaphors are still standing in the wings, the beauties in this piece far outweigh the infrequent jarring notes. It is one of Chocano's strongest epic works.

The occasion for the writing of this epic was a literary contest sponsored by the Ateneo of Lima, ostensibly to commemorate the resistance of the Peruvian troops in Arica, and actually to hasten the return of the provinces of Tacna and Arica, where the promised plebiscite still had not been held. Chocano presented his long epic *La epopeya del Morro*, which won the coveted Gold Medal and served to focus attention both on himself and on the situation of the southern border.

The original text contained almost two thousand lines, the version which Chocano permitted for his *Poesías completas* (1902). In *¡Fiat Lux!* (1908) the poet retained only some 575 lines, which shows the growth of his critical capacity. In his omission of more than fourteen hundred lines, he suppressed entire cantos and all commentary not intimately connected with the central deeds.[17] Thus the anecdotes have been sacrificed for the esthetic essence and to the considerable improvement of the work. The poet of twenty-four became entangled in useless recrimination of the enemy; the poet of thirty-three removed his extreme anti-Chilean material, without in the least watering down his strong patriotic tone.

El Derrumbe, the second triumph of 1899, is the lyric outpouring of the emotion Chocano experienced from his first contact with the Peruvian mountains and jungles. Peru is divided sharply into three geographic regions of striking contrast: the mild sands of the coast, cradle of transplanted Spanish culture; the *sierra*, towering peaks and plunging valleys of the Andes; the *montaña* or *selva*, wild, tropical jungles beyond the eastern side of the imposing mountains. Leaving his coastal oasis for the first time, Chocano had been stunned by the strength and magnificence of the interior of Peru, diametrically opposite to his own *limeño* environment. Perhaps he would never have been more than the unequal singer of his earlier works if it had not been for the impact of this powerful manifestation of nature on his receptive spirit.

Indeed, this poetic work is Chocano's first great explosion of metaphors. On nearly every line the poet has lavished images, comparisons, and similes of all classes, resulting in an almost overpowering sense of tropical lushness. It is also the first of Chocano's vast *indigenista* work, his own romanticized concept of the Indian.

El Derrumbe tells the story of an Indian chief who dreams of holding all the tribes in his hand, "like a quiver of arrows." Instead, he follows a missionary priest out of the jungle and into civilization. He comes upon the daughter of a colonist and is struck with an impossible desire for this fair and innocent young girl. Later, when he hears that she is the wife of another, he flees the civilization which has only taught him to yearn for what he cannot have. He returns to his own environment. Shouting that his name is Apu-Inca, not Juan Santos, he hurls the missionary to the ground and rages that he is responsible for taking him from his nest, for filling him with false love, for humilliating him. The final fourteen lines tell us that Juan Santos Atahualpa died a great warrior, and before his death he had all the tribes in his hand, "like a quiver of arrows."

Some have called this an epic work, but the dazzling array of metaphors and the sudden passages of sheer beauty—which far outweigh the narrative of the central figure—proclaim its lyricism.

The opening poem, "El salmo de las cumbres" (The Psalm of the Peaks), conveys the majestic solitude of the mountains. "Silence and peace. The mountain ... is a titan with two hands joined together in an attitude of Christian prayer." The mountains have opened for a river to flow through, "a limpid part among dark tresses, sometimes with a net of verdure to cover the bareness of the waters." In the far horizons, "with feet of iron and heart of brass," the train passes, crossing from tunnel to tunnel "like a needle sewing mountains." The Canto "Corazón de montaña" (The Heart of the Jungle) speaks of the forest murmurs, the hum of the insects, the palpitation of a leaf, the lake who "contracts her wrinkled face." A saintly friar appears in the primitive jungles, "his cowl the profile of a mountain peak that moves." "A hundred

sparrows wheel in circles, as if they were a necklace with wings."
The spray from a waterfall "is like a bride's white veil unfurled in
the wind." "The bridge, like a savior, opens its arms and offers
redemption from the abysses." The voluptuous moon "drops her
tender kiss on the face of the brooding mountain, like a flower over
a sepulcher." "The night received the sacramental hosts of the
moon." The pool of blood "reflected the face of that savage, as if it
had been a conscience."

Chocano's use of the Indian element begins with this work and
continues through the last volumes of his poetry. From the start it
is a romanticized vision in which the Indian is seen in epic propor-
tions, always as a great warrior or a legendary Inca. Here the
Indian has reacted against the white man, yet the Spanish priest is
a radiant, self-sacrificing figure, equally compelling. The sonority of
the verses is not in accord with the sober tone of the Indian; it is
the Spaniard who is speaking. In later years, this incomplete vision
of the Indian will alienate many.

El Derrumbe, like *La epopeya del Morro*, underwent a drastic
reduction. Chocano inserted the work in *Alma América* in 1906,
retitled "El Derrumbamiento," and from some fourteen hundred
lines of the original Lima version in 1899, he saved slightly less than
one half (672 lines).

The identical subtitle to *La epopeya del Morro* and *El Derrumbe:
poema americano* (An American Poem) reveals once more the poet's
conscious intent to display an American scene, even though both
works were set locally in Peru. His future epic-lyric vision will
widen to include all of Latin America.

After the poetic growth so evident in the last two works comes
the disappointing *El canto del siglo: poema finisecular* (1901).
Chocano's first offering in the twentieth century purports to be a
tribute to the marvelous accomplishments of the century just past,
and a prophecy of future glories.

The four Cantos are cast in semiepic tone. Canto I, which is
devoted to Napoleon, is generally tiresome except for the expressive
lines: "Liberty could have been your wife; she became only your
mistress." Canto II, the best of this work, is devoted to the
independence of Spanish America and is an antecedent to his
future *Ayacucho y los Andes*. Chocano closes this section with an
affirmation of Latin America's allegiance to Spain, the mother
country, and thus expresses one of the fundamental attitudes of

Modernism. The pretentious Canto III lauds the scientists of the
century and the wonders of their discoveries. The poet foresees the
great future of aviation, cinematography, X-rays, and so on.
Canto IV, "The Last Vision," is a hodgepodge of material where we
almost lose sight of the fact that it is poetry. In describing the
future stretching out ahead he says: "What soul is not anxious to
see, if he is not blind,/rather than this corrupt democracy, the
Greek intellectual aristocracy."

It would be preferable to think that this inflated piece came
before the two works of 1899, both so superior in expression and
inspiration. Unfortunately, *El canto del siglo* represents a retro-
gression. At this stage in Chocano's development it would be
impossible not to find some happy literary figures, but as a whole
the poetry offers little of artistic value, particularly Canto IV.

In spite of the acclaim of his invariable admirers, Chocano
himself did not seem to have too high a regard for this presumptuous
undertaking of his twenty-sixth year. He included it in his *Poesías
completas* of the following year, but omitted it entirely from both
Los cantos del Pacífico (1904) and *¡Fiat Lux!* (1908), the anthologies
of his youthful work.

In fact, only five lines have been salvaged from the vast array in
El canto del siglo. Closing Canto II, they plead for Spain to shelter
him in her arms and to renew the knot of old ties, for when a ring
of gold is smashed into pieces, it is no longer a ring, but it is always
gold. Chocano will repeat these lines in his "Ofrenda a España"
(An Offering to Spain) of *Alma América*.

IV *Collections of Poetry*

Chocano published a small volume of twenty-one poems in
Guatemala, in 1901, to show his appreciation for the effusive
welcome he had received in that country. *El fin de Satán y otros
poemas* is a simple collection, devoid of the usual mottoes. Instead
of a prologue, there is a sentence quoted from the Spanish writer,
Leopoldo Alas ("Clarín"): "Chocano sings with inspiration
worthy of Quintana, when Quintana was truly inspired!"

Most of the poems come from *Selva virgen*, although Canto I,
"El águila imperial" (The Imperial Eagle), is included from *El
canto del siglo*. Five new poems appear in a section entitled "Postdata." Among these is the beautiful sonnet "Sol y luna" (Sun and
Moon), which Chocano carried into his anthologies of 1904 and 1908:

Sol y luna

Entre las manos de mi madre anciana,
la cabellera de su nieto brilla:
es puñado de sol, áurea gavilla,
oro de sol robado a la mañana.

Luce mi madre, en tanto, espuma vana,
que la ola del tiempo echó a la orilla,
a modo de una hostia sin mancilla,
su relumbrante cabellera cana.

Grupo de plata y oro que, en derroches,
colmas mi corazón de regocijo,
no importa nada que el rencor me ladre;

Porque, para mis días y mis noches,
¡tengo el Sol en los bucles de mi hijo
y la Luna en las canas de mi madre!

Sun and Moon

Between my aged mother's hands gleam bright
Her grandson's locks; they seem a handful fair
Of wheat, a golden sheaf beyond compare—
The sun's gold, stolen from the dawn's clear light.
Meanwhile her own white tresses in my sight
Shed brightness all around her in the air—
Foam of Time's wave, a sacred glory rare,
Like spotless eucharistic wafers white.

O flood of gold and silver, full and free!
You make my heart with gladness overrun.
If hatred barks at me, what need I care?
To light my days and nights, where'er I be,
In my child's curls I always have the sun,
The moon in my dear mother's silver hair!

translation by Alice Stone Blackwell

Chocano's *Poesías completas* appeared in 1902, with a prologue by his countryman Manuel González Prada. *Iras santas* is included in its entirety. The ninety poems in the original *En la aldea* have been reduced to seventy-eight, including one or two whose titles the poet has changed and a few in which he has suppressed several stanzas.[18] All twelve poems of *Azahares* appear. One poem has been suppressed from *Selva virgen*.[19] The complete and original versions of both *La epopeya del Morro* and *El Derrumbe* remain, as does all of *El canto del siglo*.

The inevitable mottoes grace the title page, and this time the Spanish wording from *Selva virgen* is changed slightly to mean: "In my art all *schools* fit as in a *sunbeam* all the colors of the spectrum," the form to which he will adhere in future works.

In his prologue González Prada discusses Chocano's poetic growth. He calls the poet a young rebel who appeared thundering out revolutionary hymns—instead of sighing with love—and managing these imprecations as no one had in Peru and few in America. Sustaining the merits of *Iras santas* even more, González Prada states that these furious attacks made him think of the Argentine Mármol anathematizing the dictator Rosas, or the Ecuadorian Montalvo clamoring for the extinction of the tyrant García Moreno.[20] High praise indeed from a person of González Prada's category! He stresses the precocity of the very young man who wrote the first two works—really a boy rather than a man—and he admires the effortless ability to paint and describe, the variety of forms and diversity of style, the freshness and originality of his developing imagination. He concludes that if some men live in a state of grace, Chocano lives in a state of poetry. The acclaim the poet has already received (and the brilliant future he predicts) are well merited according to González Prada, particularly because this poetry has flowered in the midst of the shallow intellectual progress of his country. Therefore Chocano owes everything to himself alone. As long as no one arises to eclipse his work, González Prada will call him "The National Poet of Peru."

Los cantos del Pacífico: poesías selectas (1904) is Chocano's first true anthology, which he culled from his previous work with the exception of three poems among the eight in "Postdata."[21] The process of rigid selection has begun. There are only six poems from *Iras santas*, twenty remaining from *En la aldea*, and six from *Azahares*. From eighty compositions of the last edition of *Selva virgen*, only forty-three appear. There is nothing from *La epopeya del Morro*, *El Derrumbe*, and *El canto del siglo*. Nor does the volume open with any of the mottoes so dear to Chocano.

This severe selection corresponds to Chocano's first trips out of Peru—that is, to Central America and Colombia. The poet apparently wanted to stress his objective art, his own Americanism, as evidenced by national and continental themes contrasting with the cosmopolitan and subjective poetry of Rubén Darío. Always aspiring to wield the scepter in the American scene, he must have been spurred on by Rodó's famous verdict that Darío was not the poet of America.[22] A few of Chocano's poems of the "Postdata" imply that he himself represents the *pueblo*, and even that he is the incarnation of objective and social art—false propositions. Darío and Chocano may have been two completely different temperaments, but they are alike in their inability to become part of the people. Not even Chocano's burning desire to be known as the "Poet of America" could change this.

The anthology *Los cantos del Pacífico* (1904) affixes the formal signature terminating Chocano's early period of literature. It is a subjective, extravagant, blustery period, during which—especially at the beginning—imagination and emotions run rampant. All the traits of Romanticism are abundantly in evidence. In one or two of the initial works there is a certain flavor of the opera, with an arrogant twirling of the mustache. Out of this youthful euphoria certain marked trends emerge which will characterize all of Chocano's poetry.

The initial attitude of Chocano's youth was one of protest, sometimes anarchic, sometimes organized protest. The latter either lacked concreteness, or Chocano decided upon a more advantageous setting for these personal qualities. By the time of his successful *La epopeya del Morro* he had evolved a powerful epic strain which remained one of the enduring characteristics of his poetry. Similarly, his youthful and sweet vision of nature ripened into the agitated, selvatic beauty of *El Derrumbe*. From that time, the self-styled singer of nature's magnificence considered Latin America as his own.

Chocano's first work, *Iras santas*, had kindled a languid public with emotion, but it was limited to local sentiment. Flicking off much of its false rhetoric and widening his lenses for a broader view, Chocano's art extended and increased, without necessarily becoming deeper. The metaphors were more intricately painted, the figures were more vivid and imaginative. Into his essential Romanticism crept other influences, chiefly from Modernism, although Chocano always remained the least representative of the Modernists. Around the beginning of the new century Chocano decided to call himself an "objective poet." He is a descriptive poet and certainly not contemplative, but even his most enthusiastic supporters cannot find very much of the genuine Parnassian in his work.

It is evident that Chocano progressed consciously and with the purpose of enhancing his own image. A comparison of the original *El Derrumbe* and *La epopeya del Morro* with their final 1906 and 1908 versions, respectively, clearly indicates the degree of change in the poet. Chocano's artistic progression is undeniable. He came to understand that he must curb his gushing inspiration, that he must have more artistic control of his emotions. The result is the change from unchecked spontaneity to artistry, the climb from *Iras santas* to the approaching pinnacle of *Alma América*.

CHAPTER 3

The Triumphant Poet

ALMA AMÉRICA: *poemas indo-españoles* (Soul of America: Indo-Spanish Poems, 1906) is the harvest from the seeds that Chocano scattered in his earlier works. The poetry has reached artistic maturity. In a torrent of metaphoric verse—a tremendous flowering of imagination—the poet sings of the beauties of the American Continent; but it is a controlled song now, channeled and directed by a consummate artist.

With pride Chocano opens the pages of his first book offered to a Spanish audience. The symbols of continental strength and beauty file by tinged with the glow of the poet's words—resplendent Incas, condors soaring proudly above vast spaces, thundering cataracts, shining conquerors, immense Andean peaks, boas, alligators, tropical forests, elegant viceroys, silent, barren punas. For the rapt Spanish readers this was indeed America, and Chocano was the "Poet of America" who had come to Spain to sing his savage and exotic odes of the New World. In America, and particularly in Peru, they basked in the reflected glory of their emissary.

I *The American Scene in* Alma América

Chocano displays his poems without any fixed order, spreading open a fan of multicolored work. Yet we can see certain dominant patterns. From the rich and variegated elements in this poetry, it is always Chocano's vision of the American setting which predominates.

THE CONQUEROR AND THE CONQUERED. Scenes from the Conquest form the backdrop of this bold canvas. The poet paints a glorious past and uses the epic spirit of his art to surround the Conquest with an aura of exultation.

He catches the stirring, exciting spirit of the Conquest in the unforgettable "Los caballos de los conquistadores" (The Horses of the Conquerors), probably the most famous poem of this collection. The surging, insistent rhythm marks the clatter and pawing of the horses' hoofs as they traverse mountains and valleys—manes flying and heads erect—in conquest of a New World.

> ¡Los caballos eran fuertes!
> ¡Los caballos eran ágiles!
> Sus pescuezos eran finos y sus ancas
> relucientes y sus cascos musicales.
> ¡Los caballos eran fuertes!
> ¡Los caballos eran ágiles!

> ¡No! No han sido los guerreros solamente,
> de corazas y penachos y tizonas y estandartes,
> los que hicieron la conquista
> de las selvas y los Andes:
> los caballos andaluces, cuyos nervios
> tienen chispas de la raza voladora de los árabes,
> estamparon sus gloriosas herraduras
> en los secos pedregales,
> en los húmedos pantanos,
> en los ríos resonantes,
> en las nieves silenciosas,
> en las pampas, en las sierras, en los bosques y en los valles.

> ¡Los caballos eran fuertes!
> ¡Los caballos eran ágiles!

> Un caballo fué el primero,
> en los tórridos Manglares,

> . . . .
> Y es más digno todavía
> de las Odas inmortales,
> el caballo con que Soto diestramente
> y tejiendo sus cabriolas como él sabe
> causa asombro, pone espanto, roba fuerzas
> y, entre el coro de los indios, sin que nadie
> haga un gesto de reproche, llega al trono de Atahualpa
> y salpica con espumas las insignias imperiales.
> ¡Los caballos eran fuertes!
> ¡Los caballos eran ágiles!

> Oh! the battle-steeds were mighty!
> Oh! the battle-steeds were nimble!

Their haughty necks were slender
And their broad breasts silken, shining!
Oh! the battle-steeds were mighty!
Oh! the battle-steeds were nimble!

Not alone great warriors were they
With bright breastplates, helmets, standards,
They who made the mighty conquest of the forests
    of the Andes,
Twas the steeds of Andalusia
In whose blood, nerves, Arab sparks burn,
They sealed glory of their great race
On the pebbly lava,
Jungles,
On the forests,
On the silent, snowy mountains,
On the "pampas," on the "sierra,"
On the groves and on the valleys.

    Oh! the battle-steeds were mighty!
    Oh! the battle-steeds were nimble!
      from the translation of Edna W. Underwood
      "The Arab Steeds of the Conquerors"

The same stirring note of heroic endeavor is sounded in "Lo que dicen los clarines" (What the Bugles Say): the call of the Spanish trumpets heard over the solitary Andean peaks, the shining summits, the indifferent pampas, the curling rivers, the luxurious forests. "Oh the resounding ambitions that stun the heights! In the souls of the grandchildren of these Spanish heroes there are three centuries of zeal, three centuries of weariness." In Chocano's eyes the figure of the Conqueror is always radiant, super-heroic, the everlasting pride of Spain. Poem after poem celebrates the luminous quality of the courage and daring of these "Conquerors of Life."

The figure of the Indian is no less majestic than his conqueror. Indeed, the poet's vision of the Indian always embraces the sumptuousness of the Inca throne, the grandeur of a lost empire. Only the exotic and the picturesque really concern Chocano in all his enormous historic and legendary indigenous material. The reader is often dazzled by this fantastic empire, as in "La tierra del sol" (Land of the Sun), Chocano's poetic synthesis of Peruvian history; (Forty thousand slaves open the way for the Inca to pass

from Cuzco to Cajamarca; the young Indian maids weave dances
in front of the procession, the gleaming soldiers behind, "the Inca,
enveloped in gold, seems a vision." The sun quickens the road into
flames, and "like a boa with gleaming scales, the slow procession
unwinds"):

> Cuarenta mil esclavos abrieron el camino
> del Cuzco á Cajamarca, por donde el Inca va;
> su padre, el Sol, le alumbra; y el regio peregrino
> devora millas, leguas . . . Y siempre más allá.
>
> . . . .
>
> Tejiendo muelles danzas las indias van delante;
> detrás van los soldados de aspecto fulgurante;
> el Inca, envuelto en oro, simula una visión.
> Y sobre aquel camino, que el Sol aviva en llamas,
> como lo hiciese un boa de fúlgidas escamas,
> se va desenroscando la lenta procesión.

Entwining both cultures of the Conquest, the poet composes
many tales of thwarted romances. "La Ñusta" (The Inca Princess)
—with fine epic tone that is restrained and controlled—is the story
of an Inca princess and a Spanish conqueror. It is an impossible
love, for although the Conqueror offers his noble name, his country,
and his God to the princess, for her he is still the enemy. She loves
only the Inca Hualpa-Cápac. In anger the Spaniard has the Inca
captured and imprisoned; and since the princess refused his
honorable offer, he now forces her to pay with her virtue for the
privilege of seeing her beloved once more before his death. The
ñusta, daughter of a proud race, rubs poison over her lips, and thus
slays her violator, the Inca, and herself. Yet in death it is the
Conqueror who triumphs, for she is buried at his side. "There is no
Spanish soul who does not succeed in his intent!"

The same controlled mastery of the subject is seen in "El
Derrumbamiento," the pruned version of *El Derrumbe* (where the
romantic roles are reversed from those of "La Ñusta"). Chocano
has learned the wisdom and the artistry of compressing a tale into
defined limits, and the strength and beauty of his lyric-epics are no
longer marred by the clutter of extraneous material.

In many poems Chocano recounts the deeds of celebrated heroes
of the indigenous race. The Aztec Cuacthemoc smiles in his
torment—"My bed is not of roses"—and in silence is consumed by

flames without revealing the secret of the treasure.[1] Caupolicán, an Araucanian, carries a huge tree trunk for three days in an endurance contest. He dreams he sees his race under a yoke, and therefore on the third day he heaves off the trunk, which sinks into the ground to form his pedestal.[2] A sonnet to the Incan Cahuide pictures this solitary warrior leaping from the heights of his stone fortress rather than allow himself to be captured by the Spaniards.[3]

The poet of Lima is always aristocratic by nature, and if he uses an indigenous theme it must deal with an Inca, or a great warrior. On the surface Chocano pretends to admire the "haughty race," and bursting with poetic emotion he often proclaims himself the son of the Inca! It would be a gross error of judgment, though, to take the poet's words at face value. Perhaps he did believe that he possessed some of the strength and audacity inherent in the Inca empire. However, this *limeño* wished no one to assume that his pure Spanish heritage had been tainted by the blood of the Indians in their contemporary state of degradation! Actually "Chocano, colonialist soul, uses the Indians in the same way as the conquerors, in order to elaborate his own empire of colorful compositions."[4]

In *Alma América* the resplendent, arrogant Chocano consciously set about creating a picture of himself. The Conquest served him admirably, for he could mingle the valiant Spanish conqueror and his magnificent foe. Chocano belonged innately to the Spanish realm. Being aligned, also, with the heroic and sumptuous Inca empire only made him seem more exotic to the Europeans; and his careful distinction of legendary characteristics and his gilded vision of an ancient civilization did not offend the aristocracy of Lima. His triumph was secure in both the Old and the New World.

NOSTALGIA FOR A GLORIOUS PAST. The spiritual and intellectual formation of Chocano belonged to Lima, and the poet captured her spirit and always saw life through her eyes. The "City of Kings" has no roots in an indigenous past because it was Spanish sap which nourished this decorative Iberian transplant. Of Spanish family and Spanish cultural outlook, Chocano inherited their vanity and nostalgia for the glory of the past when Lima was the golden city of the Viceroyalty. "Oh age of the Viceroys that has never been equalled" is a frequent lament in Chocano's poetry.[5] In verse after verse the poet of Peruvian inspiration speaks with longing of the noble and proud capital. "Ciudad colonial" (Colonial City) expresses his nostalgic emotions;[6] (The remembrance of the

Viceroyalty causes him to sigh, "Oh elegant sadness." The winding
streets, the ancient balconies, the archaic porticos with their stone
escutcheons, the Cathedral—all recall the past glory of Lima, so
superior to the pale reflection of the Lima in his own time):

> ¡Oh Ciudad de los Reyes! . . .
> va á cantarte el Poeta, que el Virreinato evoca
> con el llanto en los ojos y el suspiro en la boca;
> porque extraña ese tiempo de primor y nobleza:
> ¡Oh dolor blasonado! ¡Oh elegante tristeza!
>
> . . . .
>
>   Las callejas tortuosas, los vetustos balcones,
> los arcaicos portales con sus pétreos blasones,
> tu Catedral . . .
> ¡Oh Lima! ¡Oh dulce Lima! Ciudad de los amores:
> en ti sí que los tiempos pasados son mejores.
> Retrato de hace un siglo: tú sabes propiamente
> que es un fantasma apenas la Lima del presente.

"El palacio de los virreyes" (The Palace of the Viceroys) has the
same nostalgic flavor. Sadly the poet laments that in the old
palace where elegant viceroys gravely offered their arms to
charming ladies, democratic laws are now being imposed (like an
elephant foot crushing a flower). "Oh who would not wish to
return to those centuries of valor and gracefulness! . . . Is it not true
that this useless freedom brings sadness?"

Although the depth of such a nostalgia can be questioned,
Chocano does seem less artificial in this vein of writing. "Longing
for the past and scorn for the existing scene are the innermost
thoughts of the ever-present colonialists and Perricholists of Lima,
and since this is an essential part of the character of any *limeño* the
conscious desire for effect is not so blatant as in some other poems."[7]

The poet possesses a dynamic sense of tradition, so that the past
becomes animated and dramatic. Many aspects of the colonial
epoch reach out to inspire Chocano. ("The age of the Viceroys is a
dance of great brillance."[8]) Graceful sonnets speak of the richness
and elegance of those days: "El paseo de aguas" (The Promenade
of the Fountains), "La espada de virrey" (The Viceroy's Sword),
"Alameda colonial" (A Colonial Park). The ironic "La Tapada"
(Veiled Woman of Lima) contains the spicy fragrance of a *Tradición*

by Ricardo Palma. The viceroy enters the city and is smitten with the half-hidden charms of the *tapada;*[9] but the price of this illicit love is death for the Viceroy and a convent for the faithless wife. With the picaresque sting in the *limeña* manner the poet concludes: one of her eyes has caused such unrest, but think "if instead of one, she would unveil both!"

The sight of old cities brings forth a musing quality of nostalgia in the poet. "Ciudad vieja (Antigua Guatemala)" (Ancient Guatemala City) describes the peace of that motionless city, the ancient houses with creaking doors, the tiled roofs choked with faded moss, piled refuse lying in the streets, deserted plazas asleep in the sun. The sonnet closes on a philosophical note, usually not found in Chocano's poetry. "Historic city ... you possess the greatest human happiness; to live indifferent to everything."

The sense of the hushed past of an older civilization is equally haunting. "Momia incaica" (Inca Mummy) is one of the most moving poetic works in this collection, devoid of affectation, yet overflowing with emotion. Here the vast splendor of the Inca empire is shrouded with infinite sadness, because it is finished, because there is nothing left: "Final vestige of a glorious past/I see you as a fatal lesson/in a museum, and at your side/the armor of your Conqueror."

Many of the triumphant banners of *Alma América* will be torn down in the future, but the one waving for Chocano's talent to evoke the past will be respected. Standing before the ruins of an Inca temple Chocano feels he has been born too late. "Poet. Sing of the Past. For that you have been born."[10]

CONTINENTALISM. Yet this poet, so drenched with yearning for the past, is at the same time the voice of continental destiny. "Ciudad moderna" (A Modern City) is a tribute to a strong, triumphant city looking to the future: "Buenos Aires, who assures a country for all, is the expectant mother of the Future Race." "El canto del porvenir (palabras internacionales)" (Song of the Future: International Words) is Chocano's prophecy of future continental glory. He speaks of a period of expansion when the United States "with athletic hand" will produce wonders from engineering skills, opening up the rich Amazon area. The climate will force the blond race to retreat to its cold north, but the flourishing Latins, pouring in from all over the world, will rise up and challenge "the States, no longer United." At a distance, an armed Japan looks upon a young, free, fertile country of the Amazons, the center of the world!

"La epopeya del Pacífico (á la manera yanki)" (Epic of the Pacific: in the Yankee Manner) extols the feats of the United States, but with that typical reserve toward the Saxon which really masks a basic fear. If Spanish America wishes to be free, then Chocano tells her to imitate the United States first and afterwards become her equal. While he admits that the Latin American should distrust the man with blue eyes, he believes there is no need to fear a future conquest because the South American forests "know no better race nor do the Andes know the importance of being white." Strong concluding passages assert that the blond race may open the way through the isthmus, but it will be dark heads who gather the fruits.

Some critics have tried to base a kind of Pan Americanism on occasional lines in the poetry. To Chocano the Isthmus of Panama is the symbol of union and peace "making of the two oceans but one";[11] and in his personal design for the Continent's destiny he acknowledges that "Adam came from the North, Eve was Latin."[12] But these ideas are the closest the poet ever comes to approximating anything like a Pan American spirit. Never contemplative, Chocano advocates action to herald the coming of a great Latin America. While this poetry might be said to embody a continental patriotism or solidarity it can hardly be stretched to include Pan Americanism![13]

THE BEAUTY OF THE CONTINENT. Poem after poem in *Alma América* glorifies the natural beauty of the Continent. Indeed much of the poet's fame rests upon the luxuriant and glittering qualities of his descriptions which came to be the hallmark of Chocano's poetry. Consider the flights of imagination in the following sonnets:

Los Volcanes

Cada volcán levanta su figura,
cual si de pronto, ante la faz del cielo,
suspendiesen el ángulo de un velo
dos dedos invisibles de la altura.

La cresta es blanca y como blanca pura:
la entraña hierve en inflamado anhelo;
y sobre el horno aquél contrasta el hielo,
cual sobre una pasión un alma dura.

Los volcanes son túmulos de piedra,
pero á sus pies los valles que florecen
fingen alfombras de irisada yedra;

y por eso, entre campos de colores,
al destacarse en el azul, parecen
cestas volcadas derramando flores.

The Volcanos

Every volcano rears its outlined height
As if upon a sudden o'er the sky
Fingers unseen suspended from on high
The corner of a veil before our sight.
The mountain's crest is white, and purely white;
With hot desire its heart seethes burningly.
Strange contrast is the ice to fire so nigh,
Like a stern soul above a passion's might.
Volcanos are grim stone-heaps, dark and bare;
But at their feet the blooming vales we see
Like carpets many-hued, with spangled bowers;
And there, amid those fields of colors fair,
Outlined against the blue, they seem to be
Baskets o'erturned, that pour abroad their flowers.

translation by Alice Stone Blackwell

In speaking of the vast *punas* of Peru, those barren plateaus
stretching over the Andes, Chocano says:

Las Punas

Silencio y soledad ... Nada se mueve ...
Apenas, á lo lejos, en hilera,
las vicuñas con rápida carrera
pasan, á modo de una sombra leve.

¿Quién á medir esa extensión se atreve?
Sólo la desplegada cordillera,
que se encorva después, á la manera
de un colosal paréntesis de nieve.

Vano será que busque la mirada
alegría de vívidos colores,
en la tristeza de la puna helada:

sin mariposas, pájaros, ni flores,
es una inmensidad deshabitada,
como si fuese un alma sin amores.

The Puna

But silence, solitude ... No thing that lives ...
Yet dim, in line that's long, far far away,
Vicuñas with fine-fretted footing sway.
They pass ... But shadow which a shadow gives.
With sextant this bold space who'd dare to storm?
The mighty, lone, uncoiling mountain-row
Looms onward, later swells to grotesque form—
Parenthesis colossal carved of snow.

Vain, childish he whose eyes would try to gain
Leaf-gladdening with colors' varied hue
Within the sadness of this frozen plain ...
Nor butterfly, nor bird, nor flower it knew,
Immensity where man may never dwell.
And lonely as a loveless soul as well.

translation by Edna W. Underwood

When Chocano confronts the Andes he becomes eloquent in his imaginative descriptions. His portraits of nature are often exaggerated, even distorted, but the force and originality of his fantasy always reflect some aspects of reality.

Los Andes

Cual se ve la escultórica serpiente
de Laoconte en mármoles desnudos,
los Andes trenzan sus nerviosos nudos
en el cuerpo de todo un Continente.

Horror dantesco estremecer se siente
por sobre ese tropel de héroes membrudos,
que se alzan con graníticos escudos
y con cascos de plata refulgente.

La angustia de cada héroe es infinita,
porque quiere gritar, retiembla, salta,
se parte de dolor ... pero no grita;

y sólo deja, extático y sombrío,
rodar, desde su cúspide más alta,
la silenciosa lágrima de un río.

The Andes

Like Laocoön's sculptured serpent
of marble bare, the Andes twine
their mighty knots along the spine
of an entire Continent.

Dantescan horror makes us cringe
before that throng of heroes bold,
who rise with granite shields made gold
and capped with helmets silver-tinged.

Each hero's filled with endless grief;
he longs to shout, to leap, to quiver,
is rent with pain—yet does not cry,

And somber, as his sole relief
he rolls down from the peak most high,
the silent tear of a river.

                    P. R-P.

Certainly these sonnets are exciting portrayals of natural beauty. However, Chocano's Andean landscapes never penetrate beyond these pictorial effects. For him the Andes do not speak; they shudder and writhe in silent pain. In the telluric immensity there is only emptiness and silence. We see the majestic strength of nature, but never the tragedy of the man existing there. With poignant artistry Chocano describes the sad moans of the Indian flute sending its plaintive tones over the cold punas of the Andes: "Breath of a soul become the wind/breath of the wind become a soul."[14] But why is the lament so agonizing? Chocano listens only to the tones of the instrument.

As the swan belongs to Darío, the condor is Chocano's symbol. In "El sueño del cóndor" (The Condor's Dream) the majestic bird is poised on a snow-capped peak, alone, mingling with the mists, becoming substanceless and sinking into the darkness as the soul sinks into meditation when alone. The captive bird of "El cóndor ciego" (The Blind Condor) has had his eyes removed. When he is released he flies to invisible heights, higher and higher, searching for light. Finally, understanding that he is blind and that his flight is without purpose, he falls, lifeless (like a lost hope), but with his wings outstretched and his head erect. A poem beautiful in concept and beautiful in its development!

Other verses invite us to follow beyond the Andean cordillera
into the forests of the tropics. How wild and untrammeled are the
figures that surge out of that selvatic luxuriance—yawning
alligators, dragon-like iguanas, frightened herons in flight, the
coiled boa, stalking tigers and pumas, choked swamps, and in the
depths of the jungle the silken flowers.

The graceful and delicate sonnets "La Magnolia" (The Magnolia)
and "Las Orquídeas" (The Orchids) reach lyric heights. Chocano's
magnolia blooms with shimmering whiteness:

La Magnolia

En el bosque, de aromas y de músicas lleno,
la magnolia florece delicada y ligera,
cual vellón que en las zarpas enredado estuviera
o cual copo de espuma sobre lago sereno.

Es un ánfora digna de un artífice heleno,
un marmóreo prodigio de la Clásica Era;
y destaca su fina redondez á manera
de una dama que luce descotado su seno.

No se sabe si es perla, ni se sabe si es llanto.
Hay entre ella y la Luna cierta historia de encanto,
en la que una paloma pierde acaso la vida;

porque es pura y es blanca y es graciosa y es leve,
como un rayo de Luna que se cuaja en la nieve
ó como una paloma que se queda dormida.

The Magnolia

Deep in the forest, full of song and fragrance,
Blooms the magnolia, delicate and light,
Like snowy wool among the thorns entangled,
Or, on the quiet lake, a foam-flake white.

Its vase is worthy of a Grecian maker,
A marble wonder of the classic days.
It shows its fine, firm roundness, like a lady
Who with bared breast her loveliness displays.

Is it a pearl? Is it a tear? We know not!
Between it and the moon, with mystery rife,
There is some unknown story of enchantment,
In which perhaps a white dove lost its life;

For it is pure and white and light and graceful,
Like a soft moonbeam on a snowbank deep,
That rests upon the snow and mingles with it;
Or like a dove upon the branch asleep.

translation by Alice Stone Blackwell

In "Las Orquídeas" the poet spins his ideas into a graceful,
imaginative design:

Las Orquídeas

Caprichos de cristal, airosas galas
de enigmáticas formas sorprendentes,
diademas propias de apolíneas frentes,
adornos dignos de fastuosas salas.

En los nudos de un tronco hacen escalas;
y ensortijan sus tallos de serpientes,
hasta quedar en la altitud pendientes
á manera de pájaros sin alas,

Tristes como cabezas pensativas,
brotan ellas, sin torpes ligaduras
de tirana raíz, libres y altivas;

porque también, con lo mezquino en guerra,
quieren vivir, como las almas puras,
sin un solo contacto con la tierra.

The Orchids

Whims of crystal, airy trappings,
Surprising, enigmatic things,
Apollo's crown should be these blooms,
Adornments fit for regal rooms.

On knots of tree trunks they ascend,
And twist and wind their serpent stems
Until they hang from a great height,
Poised like wingless birds in flight.

Lonely, like pensive heads they're found,
Their flowers free, with no dull ties
Of tyrant root to keep them bound.

For they, at pains to prove their worth,
Desire to live like stainless souls,
Without one contact with the earth.

P. R-P.

Although Chocano's love for Peru and his sense of the Peruvian is uppermost in his portrayal of the American scene, this does not prevent the poet from considering himself the Singer of all Spanish America. His idea of continentalism, fostered by his contact with many Latin American countries, caused him to extend his verses over the frontiers and to describe the external beauties and geography of the Continent and beyond, from the Straits of Magellan and the Tierra del Fuego northward into Mexico. America inspires Chocano, and he sings to her with exuberant vitality and emotion. His public responded with fervent enthusiasm.

II *Hispanism in* Alma América

While the multihued American scene forms the core of this collection, it is possible to separate other definite qualities. Chocano's Hispanism, although not so prominent as his Americanism, stands out as a distinct element. It is a conciliatory, filial Hispanism, a genuine aspiration to unite the New World to Spain through bonds of spiritual allegiance.

His eloquent "Ofrenda a España" reflects this tone. He is the poet who has come from across the sea—perhaps on the very wave which put Columbus on the shore of an unknown continent—to offer his book, pulsating with continental life, with its idols of yesterday and the faith it now embraces. What greater tribute to Spain than to know that the Indies choose to be free but not estranged from their spiritual mother? And thus whenever Spain is troubled with doubts, she can console herself with the knowledge that a world looks to her with love and greets her in her own tongue. Chocano concludes fervently: "Oh mother Spain, shelter me in your arms . . . and renew the knot of old ties:/for when a ring of gold is smashed into pieces/it is no longer a ring, but it is always gold."[15]

The same desire for cultural reunion is seen in the narrative of "Crónica alfonsina" (Alfonsine Chronicle). Two converging ships meet on the Atlantic. In one, Dulcinea speaks of the idealism and faith she is taking to the New World; in the other, Doña Jimena describes the unsheathed sword she brings back to infuse fresh power into a tired nation. Their words inspire Don Quijote and Don Rodrigo, who, each recognizing a need in his own nature, exchange vessels and hence their destinations. Spain and the new Continent will be one.

Chocano appends the words "Chronicle of the Reign of Alfonso XIII" to the above poem. The king is also the recipient of the "Dedicatoria," three sonnets in which the poet offers his book of the American soul to the Spanish monarch—a somewhat incongruous note which did not go unnoticed by many Latin Americans. Chocano invites Alfonso to enter his forests and breathe the air of the Andes and the tropics. Although his muse is savage, she is the daughter of a Catholic queen and of the Sun, and the poet believes that monarch and muse will understand each other because Cervantes was the finest viceroy in the New World.

Spain inspires other songs. The empty iron husks in the royal armory recall the glorious deeds of Spaniards on both sides of the sea. The result is the stirring, rhythmical poem "En la armería real" (In the Royal Armory). In "En el Museo del Prado" (In the Prado Museum), thinking about his native land, the poet longs to be part of both America and Spain. Even "Pandereta" (Tambourine), written in Andalusia and the most completely Spanish in spirit, mentions: "If I am from Lima, you have been there too"; and in my blood, although distilled by four centuries, there is still a drop of Andalusian joy and vibrance.

Chocano's striving to bind the New World to the Old through ties of filial gratitude is vividly expressed in the sonnet "Seno de reina" (A Queen's Breast). What pride of race to possess a queen who gave her breast to a hungry child, as Spain gave her breast to a world! Obviously this sonnet was greatly admired in Spain. The disastrous war of 1898 had not only stripped Spain of her last colonial possessions, but had brought the psychological effects of defeat as well. Chocano's poem—an attempt to restore some measure of national pride to a disheartened nation—is undoubtedly the most magnanimous rendition available of the Conquest. However, for most modern readers the gesture of reconciliation is so sentimental and unrealistic that it destroys its effect.

III *Personal Declarations in* Alma América

The Chocano of self-glorifying assertions, although much less in evidence in this collection, can still be heard in the dramatic personal declarations. The self-styled coat-of-arms of "Blasón" (Escutcheon) proclaims his splendid heritage. Indeed this sonnet is a self-portrait, stamped with the indelible features of the poet:

Blasón

Soy el cantor de América autóctono y salvaje:
mi lira tiene un alma, mi canto un ideal.
Mi verso no se mece colgado de un ramaje
con un vaivén pausado de hamaca tropical.

Cuando me siento Inca, le rindo vasallaje
al Sol, que me da el cetro de su poder real;
cuando me siento hispano y evoco el Coloniaje,
parecen mis estrofas trompetas de cristal.

Mi fantasía viene de un abolengo moro:
los Andes son de plata, pero el León de oro;
y las dos castas fundo con épico fragor.

La sangre es española é incaico es el latido;
¡y de no ser Poeta, quizás yo hubiese sido
un blanco Aventurero ó un indio Emperador!

Escutcheon

I am the Singer of America, autochthonous
and wild. My song has an ideal, my lyre has a soul.
My verses do not sway in time sweetly monotonous
as though to gently hang from tropic branches were their goal.

When I feel I am Incan, I render to the Sun-King
my homage, and I receive the scepter of his power;
When I feel I am Spanish, of Colonial times I sing,
and out of crystal trumpets my verses seem to flower.

My rich imagination comes from Moorish stock of old;
the Andes are of silver, but the Lion is of gold;
and these two races fuse in me with sound of epic roar.

My blood indeed is Spanish, but Incaic its pulsation;
and were I not a Poet, perhaps as my vocation
I'd be a white adventurer, or Indian Emperor.

P. R-P.

In the pomp of his verses Chocano often calls attention to his exotic nature, begotten from the pride of the Incas and the ardor of Pizarro: "I am partly Precolumbian and partly Conqueror. I am doubly epic."[16] At other times he proclaims the nobility of his dual background: "How many times I have been born! How many times I have been incarnated! I am from America twice, and twice from Spain. If I am a poet now, I was a Viceroy in the past, a Captain in the Conquest and a Monarch of the Sun."[17] Above all he is a poet, with a poet's high mission: "Now I am a Poet; I am divine, I am sacred."[18] One could hardly be more self-satisfied.

His literary creed proudly insists upon his independence: "My cult is not the cult of those who preceded me"; and again, "I will search for another Muse who will astound the Universe!"[19] He candidly admits that in his song there is all grace and all vigor because the conquerors have given him their heroic splendor, and the viceroys, their lyric exquisiteness![20] But he confesses that in spite of his love for colonial pomp he prefers metals to the finest chords, and he will sacrifice his pretty trinkets like the nobles of old who gave their rings to be melted into bells. (Unamuno somewhat deflates this concept when he states that Chocano gives a metallic sound to even the finest chords. He hastens to add that he does not mean this as a reproach, only to show the strong effect of his vigorous poetry.[21])

Just once do we catch sight of a Chocano who is not the arrogant, triumphant hero. In "Bajando la cuesta" (Descending the Slope) he travels down the mountainside alone, as night falls. The horse is picking its way from stone to stone when suddenly the poet hears the happy sounds coming from a small village below him. An acute sense of exclusion, of the emptiness of a wanderer, sweeps over him: "and at that moment I think the way is sad, the horse, drooping, the slope, very long." For the optimistic poet of thirty-one this is but a momentary sensation. In later years the aroma of sadness often pervades his poetry.

Much more in keeping with the resplendent Chocano of *Alma América* is the final "El alma primitiva" (The Primitive Soul). Here the poet transmigrates his own soul into the soul of nature, which results in an outpouring of rich Chocanesque figures. He is the primitive soul of the Andes and the forests, the creaking of the tree trunks, the hymn of the waters and the winds, the howling of the beasts. Many times, deep within himself, he feels that he was once an enormous tree with gigantic roots, sheltering the jaguars of the forest. At other times he dreams of when he was a peak of the Andes on which the snow of ten centuries rested, and from his heights he could see over the vast stretches of the Continent from the pampas to the rivers at his feet. The sounds of the Continent have taught him their secrets and have added an eighth string to his lyre—the string of savage music.

Soy el alma primitiva

soy el alma primitiva de los Andes y las selvas,
Soy el ruido de las hojas en la noche,
que parece que en mis versos ensayaran una orquesta;

. . . .

Yo era un pico de los Andes,
era un pico de los Andes, el orgullo de una piedra;
y, de pronto,
sobre todos los rigores de mis nieves sempiternas,
sentí el vuelo de un gran pájaro,
sentí el vuelo de un gran pájaro en las nieblas,
que clavando sus diez garras
en mis crestas,
dió á los aires su estridente
voz de cóndor como el grito sofocado de un alerta.
Y esa voz sonó en los siglos.
Es la voz que por en medio de mis cánticos resuena;
y que dice todavía, sobre todas las edades,
recorriendo ocho sonidos en mi lira de ocho cuerdas:
¡Soy el alma primitiva,
soy el alma primitiva de los Andes y las selvas.

I am Spirit of the Andes

Primitive, soul of mountains I, of woodlands.
I am roaring of the leaves in forest-midnights,
Orchestral all my verses with the sound-sweep.

. . . .

I was summit of the Andes,
I was point and peak of stone-pride,
Of a sudden
O'er my cruel eternal snow-fields
I sensed wing-sweep over mist-heights,
Then ten claws upon my crest,
While the condor's call rang strident,
Like a war-call sad rang, stifled,
Down the centuries the sound rang,
On, on through my song it thundered,
Till today—after the ages—
it rules eight chords of my lyre.
    Primitive, I,
Soul of forests, of the Andes.

from the translation of Edna W. Underwood
"Spirit of the Andes"

IV *Characteristics of the Poetry*

Chocano's poetic repertoire ranges from formal sonnets to free verse. Although Chocano did not emphasize versification to the extent of some other Latin American Modernists, there are metrical innovations in *Alma América* acquired by study and effort. Actually these are not new in themselves, but the poet handles them with such artistic skill that they seem to be new meters. Chocano was cautious with his liberties, however, and his contributions lie mainly in the area of structural rhythms. (Chapter 4 contains a more detailed account of Chocano's versification.)

It is the outpouring of iridescent figures and images which forms the essential part of this poetry. Chocano unleashes his imagination in this collection as in no other, and his metaphors and similes stampede over one another. These are sometimes violent and overloaded, but always dazzling and of original concept. He can adjust the metaphor to suit his bold heroic epics or the imaginative descriptions of his sonnets, to express the stern beauty of "La tierra del fuego" or the gracefulness of "La Magnolia." It is a tribute to his artistry that the purely epic poems glitter with the same imagery as the shorter sonnets. If the trait of sameness can be leveled at him, of insisting that every detail be expressed in simile, it must also be admitted that the excellence and the originality of the figures in *Alma América* ward off the expected weariness. In this collection the imagery is rarely forced. Unlike his initial poetry it is only very occasionally now that the figures run away with the poet (as in "La epopeya del Pacífico" when he talks about America wrapping herself in pure sheets that will stretch out in the wind like flags of peace!) or become unduly exaggerated (as in "Ciudad conquistada" [Conquered City] when Cortés takes a step and causes the cowardly earth to tremble).

The poems quoted in this chapter contain an abundance of Chocanesque figures. Indeed, almost any poem in *Alma América* yields examples of the richness of Chocano's imagination. "The trains gallop along shaking their manes."[22] "In the reverberating distance, in the midst of the lethargy of noon, immensity opens up like a yawn."[23] When Cuacthemoc was tortured, "the fire hissed, like a stuttering plea, and tongues sprang up as though wanting to speak."[24] The condor and his mate "hovered over the winds. They were two lives and one heart throb; or two breaths."[25] "And the river gushes out, like a flock of sheep that leaves the fleece of its foam entangled on the sharp rocks."[26] In speaking of the weed-choked swamps the poet concludes: "the greenness extends over the mire, like hope over a grief."[27] The stream of melodious sounds from the flutes of the organ begins quietly, quietly, "like steps on carpets, like caressing fingers, like silk that brushes against the floor."[28]

The figures in the sonnet "El Gaucho" follow one after another. The gaucho is the pampas made man, a piece of the brave earth stretched under the sun. When he pins down the cattle, he is the arm. He unleashes his sad song as though it were a whip. His vigorous spirit stands erect over that great weariness of the earth. The yawn of the green pampas is like a fatigue that rests, or a hope that is lost.

Other aspects of Chocano's style stand out. In the manner of José Asunción Silva, an earlier Modernist, he uses the repetition of certain lines to enhance his work. "El alma primitiva," quoted in this chapter, shows the effectiveness of this technique, as does "El salto de Tequendama" (Tequendama's Leap) and "La elegía del órgano." In the latter, the opening line "The organ sounds" is repeated at intervals throughout the work, forming an expressive refrain.

Antithesis in his poetry is skillfully managed: "The village flashes all its lights:/and now it is near./The sky flashes all its stars;/and never seems so far";[29] "In the Andean mountains there is/a river, like a slithering serpent/and a lake, like a coiled serpent."[30] He is fond of stating exact numbers: "The masts of three barks, which in the distance/simulate the profile of three crosses";[31] or "across two worlds and four centuries."[32] The impression creeps in that Chocano purposely leaves nothing to the imagination of the reader, but it must be admitted that he uses this tendency of exactness with undeniable literary skill.

Chocano excels in description. His outpourings are unexpectedly restrained by his preference for the confines of the sonnet, which he sets with precise adjectives and exact rhythmic patterns. No one denies his epic spirit, which he can infuse at will into even the short space of a sonnet, for example, in "Las minas de Potosí" (The Mines of Potosí). His feeling for nature is basic to the structure of *Alma América*. He is a poet who sees the marvels of the exterior world and shouts his enormous joy. The superabundant verses of open enthusiasm, which might be called a defect, serve somehow to give a sensation of youthful force to his poetry. No longer uneven, this collection sustains the same high level throughout.

Chocano can be arrogant and despotic and still achieve gossamer effects of light and shade. Indeed this alliance of energy and delicacy, this duality of his nature, has characterized his poetic temperament from the initial *Iras santas* and *En la aldea*. In *Alma América* the vitality and enthusiasm have not departed, but the unbridled exuberance of the juvenile trumpeter has been tamed. Not all is vigor. The many beautiful and delicate sonnets sprinkled throughout this collection belie this concept: "La Magnolia," "Las Orquídeas," "Los Cocuyos" (The Glowworms), "El Añil" (Azure), "El Maíz" (Maize), "La Caoba" (Mahogony), "Las Selvas" (The Forests), "La cruz del sur" (The Southern Cross), "Pies limeños" (The Tiny Feet of a *Limeña*).

The question of lyricism in Chocano's poetry is open to debate, the verdict depending on the reader, and, in the case of formal critiques, on the era in which they were written. In his prologue to the Madrid edition, Unamuno assigns elegance, pomp, magnificence, drive, and above all, eloquence to *Alma América*. However, he doubts that Chocano should be called a lyric poet, and he adds that it is precisely this lack of lyrical quality which makes the poetry what it is—poetry which speaks to the eye and the ear, to the imagination, and to the voluptuousness of living. Unamuno calls this beautiful poetry but not spiritual poetry.

It is true that the intimate, lyric side of the poet is overshadowed in *Alma América* by the torrential outpouring of color and splendor. He is not the poet to seek for consolation in times of grief and suffering. Nevertheless the lyric aspect, seemingly undefined here, exists in many sonnets, in the haunting evocations of the past, and in the emotion felt in the presence of nature. It will take the coming years, with their inevitable measure of disappointments and pain, to sharpen and deepen this inherent lyrical quality which can be heard clearly in his last writings.

V   *The Madrid and the Paris Editions*

There were two first editions of *Alma América*, one published in Madrid, and one published a short time later in Paris. Both editions have the blessing of two celebrated Spanish American writers. Rubén Darío composed an opening "Preludio" (Prelude), whose discerning lines penetrate the qualities of his fellow poet and acknowledge the merit of this spokesman who has come "to tell us of a Continent."[33] José Enrique Rodó stamped his approval on the title page: "I recognized in you the poet who, through a rare and happy combination, unites proud boldness of inspiration with sculptured firmness of form; and who with noble design proposes to give back to poetry its arms of combat and its civilizing mission, sighting the course that in my opinion will be the path of American poetry."

Other introductory material varies somewhat from one edition to the other, although in both it is obvious that Chocano wishes to call attention to the change that has come over his poetry. There is a page for the poet's mottoes. If his initial "Either I find a way or I make one" is the typical sword-brandishing line of old, the motto immediately beneath this is a renunciation: "Consider as if not written those books which appeared before with my signature." By his rejection of previous poetry (with the exception of those poems he reserves for his next collection) Chocano means to to signify his esthetic progress, his artistic purification. The Madrid edition alone carries a phrase from Goethe, and a list of works in progress.[34]

Two final mottoes proclaim: "My poetry is objective, and in this sense alone do I wish to be Poet of America"; and repeating a former theory, "In art all schools fit as in a sunbeam all the colors of the spectrum." It seems likely that Chocano's insistence on his objectivity stems from an acute awareness of the criticism his earlier poetry had received for its turgid, overblown qualities. Actually, his claims to objectivity are refuted by his own second motto. The Paris edition has an extra page of "Salvedades" (Qualifications) in which the poet attempts to cast himself in the role of academician, discussing his use of certain contractions, accented words, internal assonances, and so on. He concludes by saying that these explanations correspond to the Parnassianism of his personal criteria of objective poetry. The remarks are of little importance, but they do show Chocano's preoccupation with being considered a formal, serious poet of his time.

The Madrid edition carries a short, personal letter from Marcelino Menéndez y Pelayo, dated April 18, 1906, in which he praises this brilliant and inspired poetry as a new link between Spain and America. A nine-page prologue by Miguel de Unamuno follows. Surprisingly, Chocano suppressed both the letter and the prologue from his Paris edition. Perhaps he was annoyed by Unamuno's reference to his lack of lyricism or by the concept of his Americanism as speaking only to the eye and the ear. However, both the prologue and the letter were highly enthusiastic endorsements.

VI   *The Impact of* Alma América

The response to *Alma América* was electric. Spanish intellectuals almost unanimously recognized Chocano as a great poet, and because of the content of this book they hailed him as "Poet of America," the title he so fervently desired. He captivated and delighted his audiences, and Madrid openly adulated this emissary from the New World.

The *limeños*, reading his poetry which was acclaimed so vocally in Spain, were flattered beyond measure. "They themselves applauded the exoticism of his Peruvian landscapes, for they were as unaware and as unconcerned with reality in the vast, isolated mountains of Perú as were the Europeans who feted the Americanism of the poet."[35]

Thus, at thirty-one Chocano was acclaimed a great poet, not only in his own country but beyond her borders, even in Spain!

The literary impact of *Alma América* was significant. The awakening of continental pride took hold of many a Latin American Modernist and turned him away from Paris toward American themes. Chocano is credited with spearheading this new direction of Modernism into channels known as *mundonovismo*, or "New Worldism." Undoubtedly, Rubén Darío must have suffered at seeing such acclaim going to another American, especially one whom they were calling "Poet of America." Darío had often proclaimed specifically that he was not a poet of the people, and he had corroborated this in his introduction to *Cantos de vida y esperanza* (Songs of Life and Hope), published the year before, in 1905. Yet even he was influenced by the popularity of American topics after *Alma América* and came to include more American material in his verse, although not in the manner of Chocano.

The tone and content of *Alma América* had literary effects in Spain, also, chiefly in a prolonged outpouring of imitative metaphors and figures.[36] Among Spanish writers we have seen that the first to voice their praises were Menéndez y Pelayo and Unamuno. If Unamuno seemed to doubt Chocano's lyric qualities, he more than compensated for this by his glowing approbations of the "brilliant visions of the American poet, sung with such sonorous and rhythmic eloquence."[37] Unamuno was so deeply impressed by Chocano's poem of the blind condor that he incorporated this figure into one of his most religious poems, "El Cristo de Velásquez" (The Christ of Velásquez), thus giving the supreme tribute of one writer to another.

VII ¡Fiat Lux!: poemas varios, 1908

Two years after the stunning success of *Alma América* Chocano published *¡Fiat Lux!*, an anthology of his youthful poems, together with new poetry. The collection ranks with *Alma América* at the pinnacle of the poet's work. We see the rigid selection, the demanding criteria, and the highest quality of Chocano's poetry. This is perhaps the only time that Chocano dedicated himself solely to polishing and organizing his work, circumstances which will not be repeated until the preparation of *Primicias de oro de Indias*, many years in the future.

Implacably the poet suppresses most of his poems previous to *Alma América*, and those which he does admit have many amputations and changes. There are five sections. Part I, "Poemas clásicos" (Classical Poems), is made up of ten compositions taken from *Selva virgen*;[38] Part II, "Poemas románticos" (Romantic Poems), comprises thirteen poems: two from the "Postdata" of *El fin de Satán y otros poemas*, four from *Selva virgen*, two from *En la aldea*,[39] and five never before published; Part III is *La epopeya del Morro*, pared from the two thousand lines of the 1899 version to only 575; Part IV, "Poemas modernistas" (Modernist Poems), contains thirty-four new poems (four will reappear in *Oro de Indias*); Part V, "Sonetos necrológicos" (Necrological Sonnets), also new, consists of five excellent sonnets dedicated to José de Espronceda.

In these last two parts the brillance of Chocano's poetic talent is clearly present. Some of his most dazzling and penetrating metaphors appear here, certainly the equal of those in *Alma América*. The "Poemas modernistas" display his repertoire of accepted Modernist meters as well as topics, and they have a somewhat softer quality rarely seen before in his work.

"Intima" (Intimate), the first selection of the "Poemas modernistas," succeeds in giving a poignant biographical account of his life, with only faint sounds of epic trumpeting. Some of the lines reveal a sensitivity usually hidden in Chocano's work. (He says he was born in the midst of war and was lulled to sleep by the harmony of the trumpets, "of which all my poetry is but an echo." He never played as a child. "No one, no one understands how old inside is a man who never played as a child." Recalling the victory of Chile over Peru he says his mother told him to listen to the trumpet of the conquerors, "and I heard it, I hear it yet. I will hear it until another greater trumpet sounds"):

> Cuando nací, la guerra
> llegaba hasta la sierra
> más alta de mi tierra . . .
> Me arrulló la armonía
> de la trompetería,
> de la que es sólo un eco toda de mi poesía;
>
> . . . .
>
> Yo no jugué de niño; por eso siempre escondo
> ardores que estimulo con paternal cariño.
> Nadie comprende, nadie, lo viejo que en el fondo
> tiene que ser un hombre que no jugó de niño.
>
> . . . .
>
> ¡Escúchalo!—decía
> mi madre . . . Y lo escuchaba, lo escucho todavía,
> lo escucharé hasta cuando resuene otro mayor.

The rest of the poem tells of his experience in prison; then of the overwhelming vision of nature that he beheld, a vision which he says returns again and again in his songs. Consider how naturally Chocano's poetry surges out of the events in his life.

In "Nostalgia" (Nostalgia) arrogance and pretense have dropped away, leaving a core of tenderness and longing: "I should like to be a tree rather than a bird,/to be wood rather than smoke;/ . . . Lord, I am tired of wandering. I am nostalgic/. . . I have lived so little! I have become so weary!"

"Baile antiguo" (An Old Dance) is a delicate sonnet rivaling Darío's work. With lyric beauty "La canción del camino" (Song from My Journey) reveals the feelings of the poet, a solitary traveler in a dark Andean night. "La novia abandonada" (The Abandoned Sweetheart) relates quite simply the story of a young girl's undying hope. "El amor mudo" (Mute Love) speaks of the impossible love of his ancestor, González de Córdoba, for his queen.

In "Crisol" (Crucible) he reiterates that he is "half Inca and half viceroy," but in a gentler tone, while in "La voz triste" (The Sad Voice) he equates his own Inca blood with the Moorish blood of a hauntingly beautiful Spanish woman. Once more in "Anacronismo" (Anachronism) Chocano laments that he was born in the present age. He confesses that he loves his country deeply, but not as she is now, rather as she was in the past. These ideas are not new, but the artistry has a deeper luster here, often shading and softening the dramatic.

It is curious that the only English writer whom Chocano mentions is Rudyard Kipling. In the poet's verse, Kipling becomes a tremendous figure. In spite of the greater sensitivity of much of this work, it is clear that the cult of the strong, the successful, the leader still surrounds the virile poet of *¡Fiat Lux!*

Two works from this collection particularly illustrate Chocano's rhythmic art: "Danza griega" (A Grecian Dance) and "La caravana del sultán" (The Sultan's Caravan). The "monorhythmical sway" of the dance is delicately conveyed by the meter of the lines; "En la caravana del sultán" uses the same rhythm to create its flowing movement. This second poem also possesses the sumptuous tones of "La tierra del sol" of *Alma América*. How Chocano loved the pomp and ceremony of such processions!

There were two editions of *¡Fiat Lux!*, the first in Madrid and the second in Paris. To account for the differences in the two we should remember the serious circumstances which surrounded Chocano in the year 1908, and his consequent need for haste. The Madrid prologue by Andrés González Blanco is scarcely nine pages long, but is expanded (unnecessarily) to ninety-five in the Paris edition. The latter also contains eight compositions at the end of the book which are not in the Madrid edition.[40]

Continuing his practice of issuing little manifestoes, Chocano states in *¡Fiat Lux!:* "My ideal in Life and in Art would be to blend the imagination of the Latin, the gravity of the German, and the energy of the Saxon." His two best-known mottoes follow on separate pages. It is interesting that Chocano dedicates this book "to the Argentine press, high exponent of the Hispanic-American mentality."

The lengthy and highflown prologue by González Blanco in the Paris edition is full of incredibly exaggerated statements which give an idea of the adulation Chocano received from some quarters.

It also reads like a defense of both the poet and his poetry and indicates that personal dislike of Chocano as well as literary criticism had seeped in over the last two years. González Blanco, however, will admit no shortcomings in his ideal poet.

Alma América and *¡Fiat Lux!* express the highest point of artistry in Chocano's work. The first is more colorful and dramatic, more charged with emotion; the second shows a sterner concept of art. Together they represent the summit of Chocano's poetic fame.

CHAPTER 4

The Modernist

NO ANTHOLOGY of the Modernist movement in Spanish America ever excludes the name of José Santos Chocano, yet his place of honor often seems grudgingly given. The great Modernists are announced with the proper awed voice, and then at the end of the guest line Chocano is presented, almost apologetically. In addition, Chocano himself stands apart from the others as though proud of his difference.

When Chocano began writing, the young and uncertain literature of Latin America was filled with the fervor of Modernism. We must know, then, what Modernism is in order to judge Chocano's rightful position in the literature of his epoch.

I *Spanish American Modernism and Its Beginnings*

Around 1880 to 1885 a fresh and youthful urge for wider artistic horizons began to show itself. The resultant wave of literary renovation which swept through Latin America came to be known as Modernism. It was an esthetic movement that had deep artistic effects on the literature, and it arose as one facet of a continental stirring and awakening.

The roots of Spanish American Modernism are found in the political and social climate of that era. The political emancipation of Latin America from Spain had plunged the new countries into social chaos, with dictators and local revolutions as the order of the day. Obviously, intellectual independence was even more difficult to attain, and long years of struggle were needed to shake off colonialism of mind and spirit. The cultured classes were made up of a small minority of persons, usually clustered in the capitals of each country, who had been educated in Europe and who certainly identified themselves with the upper classes of Spain and France rather than with the unassimilated Indians and mestizos that formed the vast majority in their native lands. This intellectual colonialism of the privileged caste led to many stultifying social attitudes and habits and contributed to unstable and irresponsible governments. As a result, Latin America remained a spiritual Spanish colony for an unduly long period of time.

Under such circumstances it was hardly to be expected that there would be an easy transition into an independent and original literary life. Nevertheless, by 1880 the writers of Spanish America did desire to be something other than displaced Castilian children. Young poets of originality, restive under the yoke of Spanish literary dominance, began to find the traditional Spanish forms too rigid and inadequate for their emotions. In each capital small groups of writers—still in need of direction—turned attentive faces to Paris. Without much confidence in themselves and with no interest in their neighbors, Spanish American cultural activity was groping, disunited, and confused. French literature seemed to offer models which would satisfy their expanding artistic desires, a predictable development considering that French influence had permeated nearly every phase of cultural life since the days of political independence from Spain.

Thus while Modernism is recognized as a distinct Spanish American literary movement, the origins of its literary forms must be sought in the development of French letters during the nineteenth century. In France, Romanticism had exhausted itself more or less by 1850, to be replaced by an objective attitude toward life and a refuge in the ivory tower. The French Parnassian poets, reacting against the emotional excesses of Romanticism, believed the two essential aims of poetry should be marmoreal perfection of form and the impersonal attitude of the writer toward his subject. The reaction against this concept of "Art for the sake of Art" came from a group of writers who felt that the vitality of literature was being destroyed by the impersonal tendencies and impeccably sculptured lines of the Parnassians. This Decadent-Symbolist reaction also had the search for beauty as its main purpose, but the attitude became more subjective, more concerned with the idea and the emotion to be conveyed. The search for self-expression often resulted in extravagant and frenzied outpourings, a reflection in itself of the dominant attitude of the social environment which was increasingly interested in the human personality. The poets' cult of beauty frequently took the form of hatred for the common thing, of search for rare sensations, for lustrous, subtle words. Certain esthetic emblems were constantly repeated—the fleur-de-lis, the swan, the peacock, warbling nightingales, princesses. Each poet looked into himself; each confused the rare with the beautiful. By 1885, Symbolism was in full sway in France. Using all the artistry of the Parnassians, the Symbolists sought to express their impressions in a manner which would fascinate and bring forth an emotional response. The symbol, the evolving of the image by suggestion, musical verse, freedom of structure, independence in matter of rhyme characterized the Symbolists.

The Spanish American writers reaching for new models combined these French elements with Spanish tradition, for fascination with French poetic expression was not a complete denial of Spain's literature. For additional inspiration the developing Modernists went to the Spanish Romantic poets, chiefly to Zorrilla and Espronceda, to the delicate post-Romanticism of Bécquer, and to Spain's Middle Ages, her ballads, and her Baroque writers of the Golden Age. In their search for new poetic modes they also explored much foreign literature (channeled for the most part through the French, and usually a translated French[1]). Into the developing literature filtered something from all the schools and movements of a complex age, a time of technological, sociological, and religious questioning.

Out of all these elements, but principally through the absorption of French influences, Spanish America was infused with new literary impulses that ultimately enabled it to discover its own personality and differentiate itself in essence and style from Spain. This amalgamation came to be called Modernism.[2] The highest accolade for Modernism is to say that it was actually a movement of literary emancipation in which the New World writers ceased to be imitative Spaniards in order to become what they really were, Spanish Americans. Although two purely indigenous genres had already appeared which were without prototypes in Europe—the Gaucho poetry of Argentina and Uruguay, and the *Tradiciones peruanas* of Ricardo Palma—Modernism was the first evidence of a Latin American turn toward cultural maturity, and with it the Hispanic nations of the New World took their first steps into world literature.

The publication of Rubén Darío's *Azul* . . . in 1888 is usually taken as a starting point for the Modernist era; but Darío himself should not be thought of as the originator of Modernism. We have seen that young and dissatisfied writers in many Latin American capitals, although isolated from each other, were all animated by the same desire for renovation. These were the so-called Precursors, really misnamed, for they were often contemporaries of Rubén Darío, writing at the same time as the date of *Azul.* . . . A better term for them would be "embryonic Modernists," for each poet in this first group possessed some of the features that came to be hallmarks of the continental movement. Manuel Gutiérrez Nájera and Salvador Díaz Mirón in Mexico, José Martí and Julián del Casal in Cuba, and José Asunción Silva in Colombia are always mentioned in this "first generation" of Modernists,[3] along with others who trod more timidly and whose names are found in detailed discussions of Modernism per se. The chief aim of these "embryonic Modernists" was to make their poetry original and an end in itself. The French influence can be seen, but the innovations were not completely and definitely established. These were notes of elegance, grace, and refinement that Darío would arrange into resplendent harmony.

Modernism was actually not a well-defined movement until the appearance of a leader: Rubén Darío. This poet possessed extraordinary poetic gifts and displayed to a much greater degree all the literary facets of his time. His *Azul* . . . in 1888 was the first flowering of the myriad seeds germinating in the Latin American literary soil since the previous decade or so. The cosmopolitan spirit of this work was needed in Spanish America and gave direction to the sporadic efforts of writers in many Latin American countries.

A chronological study of the writings of Darío reveals that his Modernism evolved from conscious and progressive changes in his literary principles, from *Azul* . . . (1888), of Parnassian influence, to *Prosas profanas* (1896), with the additional influence of Symbolism. Darío's works and his analyses of the literary innovations were the blueprints for all the Modernists of Latin America. Indeed, the publication of *Prosas profanas* confirmed Darío's undisputed leadership, and from his influence a flourishing movement unfolded with Modernist writers on all sides. Darío's admirers and imitators of the new style founded various literary journals, which furthered the prestige of Modernism throughout the Continent.[4] In fact,

Modernism was such a fertile field of Spanish American letters that it produced several poets of the first magnitude, even though they were eclipsed, as Modernist writers, by the radiant figure of Darío. In this group belong: Amado Nervo (Mexico), Leopoldo Lugones (Argentina), Ricardo Jaimes Freyre (Bolivia), Julio Herrera y Reissig (Uruguay), and José Santos Chocano (Peru), followed by many other excellent authors of the period.[5]

These Spanish American Modernists formed their poetry out of the elements and influences of their time. They were utterly convinced that they were creating a new art by combining diverse styles, aristocratic culture, esthetic principles, and cosmopolitanism. The Modernist esthetes were proud to belong to an Hispanic generation that for the first time formed a minority dedicated solely to art. In their concept every influence could enter into the literary forms, but art must never succumb to mediocrity. While they professed to be modern, the luster of the past was always with them because of their disdain for the "bourgeois" present. This drove them inevitably to an estheticism that considered art superior to life. They learned perfection of form from the Parnassians, and from the Symbolists they derived perfection of musical composition. Their work was elegant, the cultivation of pure art. Above all, it brought a marvelous renovation of rhythmic techniques.

It is possible to distinguish two tendencies within Modernism itself. There is an earlier movement of escapism in which the poet took refuge in his ivory tower and wrote of imaginary and exotic themes. This was an artificial existence based on imitation of other literatures, and on the ignorance and rejection of any local problems such as poverty, illiteracy, and the oppression of the Indian masses. Above all, it looked toward Paris. A shift in direction came after 1898, marking the so-called second phase of the movement. In that year, because of the war between Spain and the United States, a response of filial sympathy ran through Spain's former colonies. Some poets did abandon their unreal world for this earth, at least to the extent that they acknowledged their common bonds of Spanish heritage inherent in the Hispanic soul. The Modernists writing in the latter part of the period are usually referred to as *mundonovistas*,[6] or New Worldists. Present-day scholars, however, stress the continued unity of both phases, their common estheticism, and a similarity of artistic forms. The New Worldists may have hurried

by the floating swans, but they continued to be escapists nevertheless, especially in their use of native material for purely esthetic
reasons.

II   *Modernism in Peru*

Peruvian history paralleled much of the history of other Latin
American countries. The last continental stronghold of the Spanish
had been in Peru. After they were defeated, the country was torn
by incessant rebellions and uprisings and by the overthrow of one
dictator after another—hardly a propitious time for literary
development. Although there was widespread racial and social
inequality this was actually not a basic factor at that time, since
the frequent upheavals were usually clashes of power within the
ruling class. Great wealth and great poverty prevailed, with little
or no middle class; economic feudalism resulted. As in all the
Andean countries, the lot of the Indians was the most wretched.

By contrast to the rest of the country, Lima was a beautiful,
glittering jewel, set on the mild Pacific coastline and known as the
"City of Kings." Lima had been the seat of the Spanish government
in South America, and colonial life there had sparkled with the
nobility and wealth surrounding the viceroy's palace. A courtly
society developed, one devoted to frivolity, to pomp and display,
to jesting laughter. The writers, usually educated in Spain or
France, were of aristocratic mind, with scorn for any democratic
leanings and complete disinterest in the native population.

In 1845 a strong man, President Ramón Castilla, took over the
reins of government for a number of years, which allowed a brief
respite for literary pursuits. A borrowed European Romanticism
held full sway over the young men writing at that time. There
were some minor poets from Arequipa who showed an affinity for
the nature which dominated their environment, and there were a
few epic verses here and there. But for the most part the only
thing which individualized the outpouring of Romantic verse in
Peru was a certain love of irony, a holdover from the aristocratic
court atmosphere of colonial Lima.

Ricardo Palma and Manuel González Prada stand out in the
task of forming literature in a new age.[7] Palma was the originator
of the *tradición*, a truly Peruvian contribution. Taking an historical
anecdote from colonial times, always something diminutive, he
embellished it with graceful prose which culminated in an ending

of malicious *limeña* irony. Palma was unique and left no true literary heirs. In the writings of González Prada the political and the literary were mixed, something quite common in Peruvian literature. González Prada is sometimes placed among the Precursors of Modernism, since his work does show glimmerings of the new poetry and there is a certain polish and brevity which is a relief from the Romantics. However, he never considered himself primarily a poet, and his burning concern was always the social and political problems of his country.

In 1879, Peru was plunged into the War of the Pacific, a disastrous war for Peru with repercussions for many years. Cultural life was almost extinguished, and this artistic sterility, extending into the 1890's, accounts in part for the fact that Modernism arrived later in Lima than in the other important capitals. In the late 1880's some young men were reading the new French writers, by this time usually in translation. (Verlaine read at the foot of the Andes in the midst of social unrest and upheaval!) But the influence of a prolonged Romanticism still continued, even if it no longer inspired. Peruvian Romantics wept because Lamartine wept; and they dedicated numerous poems to Napoleon, a la Hugo; and where the French and the Spanish Romantics had looked to a glorious past of their own, Peruvian poets simply dreamed.

Admiration for Rubén Darío penetrated the small world of Peruvian letters after the publication of his *Azul* . . . in 1888. However, unlike the situation in other capitals, there was really no Peruvian poet who had been anxiously searching for new modes of expression and who could be called even a tentative Modernist (exluding González Prada who never devoted himself primarily to poetry).

We can understand, then, the adulation which greeted the young Chocano upon the publication of *Iras santas* and *En la aldea* (1895). The small group which made up the cultured elite was overjoyed by Chocano's facile use of the new forms and technicalities that Modernism offered. For Peru the coming of Modernism signified her entrace into a cosmopolitan era, no matter how limited. It is no wonder that Chocano easily won his place as the leader of the Modernist movement in Peru, and he was soon surrounded by admirers and a host of imitators. His enormous popularity is due in part to the conscious fusion of the known and the new. Chocano wanted to please his public, and he understood what topics would bring the acclaim he sought. As though throwing flowers to a girl, he courted the *limeños* with his poems, flattering their colonial pride, assuring them of their noble heritage, covering up their deficiencies. He was a poet of the elite who sang of popular themes, and he was applauded by all Peru.

In every Spanish American country Modernism had its peculiar rhythm. The publication of Chocano's two initial works in 1895 marked the beginning of Peruvian Modernism, and Lima soon echoed with the poetry produced by the group around Chocano. Only one other Peruvian Modernist approached Chocano's pinnacle, his contemporary José María Eguren (1874? 1882?–1942), who displayed his own Modernist style, anti-epic, symbolistic, complex. However, Eguren's poetry reached the public several years after Chocano's impact. Other poets of the Peruvian Modernist group reflected various aspects of Modernism, but never achieved the brillancy of Chocano and Eguren. Of Chocano's generation were the poets José Fiansón, Domingo Martínez Luján, and Federico Barreto. A younger group of the succeeding years included José Gálvez, Abraham Valdelomar, Enrique Bustamante y Ballivían, Felipe Sassone, José Lora y Lora, Alberto Ureta, Leonidas Yerovi, Percy Gibson, and others. Some poets born in the 1890's experimented with Modernism but then withdrew to follow paths more of their time, for example, Juan Parra del Riego, Ricardo Peña Barrenechea, César Rodríguez, Alberto Hidalgo, and Alberto Guillén.

Peruvian literature owes a great debt to Chocano, for at a period when Peru's cultural prestige was among the lowest in Spanish America, this poet—a product of his own Peruvian environment—succeeded in commanding the respect and admiration of the great writers of his epoch. Pride in Chocano's triumph (which accompanied him into the 1920's as far as the Elmore incident) stirred many of his contemporaries and provided a stimulus for future self-confidence in Peruvian letters.

III *Chocano's Modernism*

In later years Chocano's place of honor in continental Modernism was sharply questioned. Conflicting opinions reflect the dispute: "If he is grouped with Darío and the other Modernists, it is because he was a visual poet who had learned to paint what he saw with Parnassian language. What he saw, nevertheless, was different

from the reality of the Modernists" (Anderson Imbert).[8] One step
further is the blunt verdict: "Chocano never was a Modernist poet
nor even modern" (Torres-Ríoseco).[9] Balancing statements appear
on the opposite side. "As a poet of the 'modernista' movement, he
[Chocano] is generally considered as second only to Rubén Darío"
(Elías Rivers).[10] "Chocano the fearless, proud apostle of Americanism . . . at the death of Rubén Darío is accorded by many the
privilege of wielding that master's sceptre" (Goldberg).[11]

What actually is Chocano's position in Modernism? From almost
the beginning of his work, Chocano launched a crusade against the
domination of Modernism by Parisian tastes. Clearly he himself
wished to preserve a definite independence from the coterie of
Darío's Modernist school. As early as 1896, in his own *La Neblina*,
he wrote a critical essay of Darío's *Los Raros* (The Misunderstood,
1893) in which he took the great Modernist to task: "*Los Raros* of
Rubén Darío, a brilliant prose writer, not in the least inferior to
the poet, should have merited our enthusiastic applause as artistic
coreligionists; but perhaps to the great surprise of Darío's chorus,
we emphatically censure his work for its context and for its
consequences. . . . They [Parisian writers] can and should continue
as they are, great artists, but we cannot and should not follow them;
Modernism must be Americanized among us. . . . Rubén Darío
owes us another work in which he ought to be less French and
more American."[12]

There is an interesting postscript. When Rubén Darío read this
opinion of *Los Raros* he sent Chocano a second copy of *Prosas
profanas*, and this time instead of a dedicatory inscription he penned
a verse from St. John's Gospel: "Again Peter denied, and at that
moment a cock crowed." Chocano understood the allusion. He sent
Darío a postcard with a colorful figure of the symbolic bird of
France. On the back he wrote, "My dear and admired Rubén:
The French teachers can be sure that no cock crows to me."[13] Both
these retorts were published in *La Neblina*.

Later works continued Chocano's campaign against French
influences, in both obvious and oblique references. "Flor de
Hispania" (Spanish Flower), from *Selva virgen* (1898?), laments the
fascination of Paris for young American poets, blinding them to the
beauties of the great Spanish writers. *Limeña* irony shows through
the delightful sonnet "Pomme de terre" (Flower of the Earth),
from *Alma América* (1906), which describes in accepted Modernist

terms the elegance of Luis XVI's salon. His Majesty's formal coat is a cascade of a thousand lights, and stuck in his lapel, as an insignia of his glory, appears the American flower (the potato). In "Arte sincero" (Sincere Art) from *¡Fiat Lux!* (1908), Chocano praises true art as opposed to that which is only fatuous form, and he concludes: "American art is to that of Europe/what a mountain peak is to a statue,/what an abyss is to the bottom of a crystal goblet." The theme of remaining faithful to one's race and land appears in the farewell speech he made in Puerto Rico in 1913 and in his coronation speech in Lima, 1922. Chocano's consistency argues in favor of his sincerity.

There may have been a personal desire to stand out from the other Modernists and adopt a course to suit this purpose, yet the fact remains that Chocano never felt the strong pull of Paris. He always capitalized on the wonders of the American scene, culminating in *Alma América*, and his glowing descriptions of an American nature, her myths and her legends, waylaid many a would-be Parisian American. His boasting of being a descendant of both the conqueror and the Inca may have been affectation and self-glorification, but pride in America is evident nonetheless. He is often criticized for his exterior vision, for not penetrating beyond the outer wrappings, but in all fairness to Chocano we should remember that he pointed the way to a new direction in Modernism, and he did so by standing against the strong prevailing winds of French influences at a time when Latin American cultural life was still precarious and uncertain.

In his preface to *Prosas profanas* (1896), Rubén Darío had rendered lip service to the idea that any poetry inherent in America rested in the Indian legends, but he never seemed to believe his own words. In 1906 Darío stated that Chocano was destined to be America's voice: "His muse is the representative of our culture, of our present Hispano American soul. Lugones, Nervo, I myself, seem foreigners. And above all, it is necessary to belong to one's own land."[14]

Certainly Chocano is the most thoroughly American of the Modernists. His swans were the condors and his eighteenth-century princesses, the Incan *ñustas*. He possessed the nostalgia inherent in the Modernists, but instead of sighing for afternoons in a Versailles garden he longed for the elegant past of Lima, or for a gilded autochthonous past. He made himself the official singer of the glories of America. Perhaps the Continent was waiting for contemplative eyes, but it was Chocano who noticed her and painted her portrait in unmistakable colors. These exterior notes may have been far from the center of reality, but they were American notes nevertheless. And in sounding them Chocano succeeded in awakening a dormant continental pride.

Modernist poetry was enriched by the violence of his style and even the primitivism of his vision, for this gusto and virility were needed as an antidote to the Modernist preciousness. Among the light voices of the Modernists, Chocano's strong baritone had a salutary effect.

Chocano is most .at home with the other Modernists in their common meeting ground of continental aspirations. No other Modernist is a more ardent advocate of continental solidarity, based on similarity of history, tradition, and a shared future. Like the others, Chocano's continentalism is tinged with a basic suspicion of the United States. This hostility stemmed from a legitimate fear of conquest, based on past and contemporary events, and an accompanying depreciatory attitude toward what he and the others considered the inferior cultural standards of the "brutal Saxon" ("Momia incaica"). Chocano's poems written in this vein never reach the stirring tone of Darío's "A Roosevelt" (To Roosevelt) or "Salutación del optimista" (Salutation of the Optimist) (*Cantos de vida y esperanza*, 1905), but Chocano himself was much more a man of his time than Darío, and the sum total of his poems presents a more vigorous and consistent expression of continentalism.

Filial devotion to Spain was advocated by all the Modernists after 1898, and Chocano entered fully into this aspect. His expressive verses from *El canto del siglo* (1901) precede by four and five years Darío's "Al rey Oscar" (To King Oscar) (*Cantos*, 1905) and Nervo's "Epitalamio" (Epithalamium) to Alfonso XIII, 1906. His *Alma América* is permeated with this idea. Lines in *¡Fiat Lux!* ask the youth of Latin America: "And are you not proud of your father Don Quijote and your grandfather the Cid?"[15]

The Modernists scorned the masses as being incapable of understanding beauty, and reacting against what they considered the drabness and uniformity of contemporary civilization, they climbed into ivory towers filled with fantasy and overrefined exquisiteness. In general, this withdrawal prevented them from facing the ugly aspects of life. Chocano was both attracted to and repelled by the crowd. What he really desired was a pedestal in the midst of the multitudes. He scorned the common people and certainly considered himself a superior being; yet his need for adulation led to many of the crowd-pleasing notes we have seen in his poetry, even if he refused to be a part of the throng. A poet involved in so much political strife is certainly aware of the shifting sands of his environment, and Chocano does not seem to escape so much as he blandly ignores what he does not wish to see. His ivory-towerism took the form of romanticizing the autochthonous. We cannot overcome the feeling, however, that Chocano would have been bored in his ivory tower if he had stayed there too long, and at the very least he would have raised a flag to wave over the turrets!

Chocano does veer away from what might be called the mainstream of Modernist poetry. The deluge of luxury and fantasy, the Rococo of the eighteenth century, preciousness, Oriental exoticism, and typically French and neo-Hellenistic evocations are rare in his work as he progresses. *Selva virgen* still displays nymphs and swans, but most of these figures departed as early as 1899 with his successful *La epopeya del Morro* and *El Derrumbe*. A faint tinge of preciosity remains, of course, but is usually applied to the American figures and scenes typical of Chocano. For example, he describes the condor's claws as "curved daggers wrought of ivory and gold" ("Sueño del cóndor"). He uses the American vicuña to speak about the useless sense of beauty; ("Lifting their haughty heads with puerile arrogance,/causing anguish with the curve of their slender necks,/the vicuñas seem to be, in their elegance,/endowed with the useless sense of the beautiful"):

> Retadora la testa con pueril arrogancia
> y angustiosa la curva del extenuado cuello,
> las vicuñas parecen estar en su elegancia
> dotadas del inútil sentido de lo bello.
>
> ("Las Vicuñas")

He describes the jewels, silk, and lace worn by a proud Mexican horseman ("Tríptico criollo. I. El Charro" [A Creole Triptych. I. The Horseman]). The American mountains plunging down to the sea, enveloped in mists, suggest "a lace of fever embroidered in a

dream, an anguished panorama of a fairy tale" ("Tramontando"
[Crossing the Mountains]). He uses gold and luxurious wealth to
describe the sumptuous Inca throne. His search for the rare and the
ancient and the remote ends in an autochthonous empire. The
Modernists' sensuous receptivity to beauty is always present, but
again, it is receptivity to American beauty as he sees it.

Part of the core of Modernism is the synthesis of sounds, colors,
and images, which provokes a purely esthetic response. These
aspects are outside Chocano's realm for the most part. An occasional poem reaches for this ideal, but he cannot enter Darío's
kingdom.

There is much elegance in Chocano's work, particularly in his
evocation of the colonial past, and much decorative and ornamental
sparkle, but he cannot create exquisiteness. His sonnet "Pies
limeños," for example, has many Modernist notes, but lacks the
delicate filigree of a poem like Darío's "Era un aire suave" (It Was
a Soft Air).

Pies limeños

Tus pies son hechos sólo para lucir las galas
de un baile en salón regio ó artistica floresta,
para tejer gavotas al son de blanda orquesta
y para deslizarse cual si tuviesen alas.

Yo, esclavamente, sigo tus huellas. Tú resbalas
como un perfume vago; y en tu actitud apuesta
hay algo de otros siglos y hay algo de otra fiesta
en otro jardín viejo o en otras viejas salas.

Tus pies, tus pies que evocan un baile voluptuoso
en las galanas noches de algún Virrey ardiente,
encelan mis deseos y angustian mi reposo;

y, así, con un estuche de los que te has calzado,
me haré una relojera para el reloj que cuente
las horas que transcurran distante de tu lado.

The Tiny Feet of a *Limeña*

Your tiny feet are made only to sparkle in the hour
of a dance in regal room or in artistic bower,
to weave gavottes in rhythm while a soft orchestra sings,
and to glide by gracefully as if your feet had wings.

As though a slave I follow in your footsteps.   Unaware
you slip past like a vague scent; in your fascinating air
there is something of other centuries and other balls,
in other olden gardens or in other olden halls.

Your feet, your tiny feet that a sinuous dance evoke
in the courtly nights of splendor of some viceroy intense,
enkindle my desires and my jealousy provoke.

Thus I will take a slipper from those which you have worn,
and make of it a watchcase for the watch that counts the moments
that elapse far from your side—precious time for which I mourn.

P. R-P.

To the Modernists the cult of form and music is all-important.
Chocano stepped into this area without fanfare. There is no doubt
that he possesses great flexibility of poetic talent, which he displays
in wide gamut, yet his caution in experimentation is also evident.
His chief contributions lie in structural rhythms, which he obtains
by striking arrangements of the hemistiches over a Classical base.
The drumming hoofbeats of the exciting "Los caballos de los
conquistadores," for example, are produced by the almost perfect
use of the tetrasyllabic foot (see page 68). Other poems in Chocano's
repertoire have twelve-syllable lines with the rhythmic four-four-
four groupings scattered throughout in order to create quite
different effects ("En la armería real" and "Añoranza" [Home-
sickness]). The poem "Momia incaica," in which all the lines are
of twelve syllables and every other line is acute, has its own
animated rhythm. Modernist cadences come easily to Chocano, as
"Soy el alma primitiva" and "Fuga" (Flight), which follow the
tetrasyllabic structure and the constant repetition of José Asunción
Silva's famous "Nocturno" (see page 84).

Chocano obtains splendid results in "Danza griega" with his
nine-syllable line as the rhythmic unity of the poem. The "monorhythmical sway" of the dance is delicately conveyed by a kind
of weaving in and out of these nine-syllable lines with lines of five
syllables, and the constant repetition of the initial two lines. The
use of assonance contributes to the effect of continuous, flowing
movement:

La griega baila gravemente.
La griega baila gravemente con monorrítmico vaivén.

Alza su cuerpo
como en un brindis una copa que hirviese llena de placer;
. . . .
La griega baila gravemente con monorrítmico vaivén.

"La caravana del sultán" and "Los toros pasan" (The Procession
of the Bulls), which also use the nine-syllable base, display the
same verbal art.

Chocano could compose a poem with the flavor of Bécquer, as in
the sensitive "De viaje." He cultivated the Alexandrine in French
style. In "La epopeya del Pacífico" he attempted ternary movement in his Alexandrine verse. The seventeen-syllable line, broken
into seven-five-five groupings, is peculiarly Chocano's ("Ante las
ruinas" [Standing before the Ruins] and "El tesoro de los Incas"
[The Treasure of the Incas]). He added to the prestige of mono-
rhyme verse, using it in eight- eleven- and twelve-syllable lines. He
refurbished the old Castilian eight-syllable meter, as in "Cinegética"
(The Hunt) with all acute lines. He attempted free verse. He
increased the combinations of lines with differing numbers of
syllables.

But while his facile use of the new versification is abundantly
evident, it is also true that this resulted in little that was daring or
original. This is not to take away from the music and especially the
rhythmic art in his poetry (nor to disregard the striking onomatopoetic effects), but to point out that in the area of versification
Chocano is definitely a follower. He cannot rival Darío's internal
rhyme nor his artful alliteration, much less the excellence of
Darío's musical verse. Chocano was not a careless writer, nor
uninformed, but he wrote too rapidly to be noted for metrical
innovations, and he did not put his greatest emphasis on versification. While he tried out many of the new techniques, he never used
them to the extent of blurring his personal verve.

It is not correct, however, to imply that Chocano had no regard
for the formal aspects of Modernism. Many careful and studied
touches reveal his knowledge of the poetry of all his contemporaries,
and his admiration for Darío's work is evident even if he wished to
carve out his own territory. As early as 1893 he had dedicated his
"Sermón de la montaña" to Darío. He consciously followed many
of Darío's directives in versification as well as ideas, often quite
flagrantly as though inviting a comparison. In *Alma América*

Chocano composed a sonnet which has the identical title of Darío's "Caupolicán" from *Azul* . . . and describes the same feat by the Araucanian Indian hero. Chocano's sonnet is a deliberate imitation of Darío's earlier work, including the Alexandrine verse and the exact consonantal rhyme scheme with acute lines in the same pattern. The Spanish reader will probably agree about the greater ease of Darío's musical verse, but each must determine for himself which sonnet leaves the stronger image.[16]

Caupolicán

Es algo formidable que vió la vieja raza;
robusto tronco de árbol al hombro de un campeón
salvaje y aguerrido, cuya fornida maza
blandiera el brazo de Hércules o el brazo de Sansón.

Por casco sus cabellos, su pecho por coraza,
pudiera tal guerrero, de Arauco en la región,
lancero de los bosques, Nemrod que todo caza,
desjarretar un toro, o estrangular un león.

Anduvo, anduvo, anduvo. Le vió la luz del día,
le vió la tarde pálida, le vió la noche fría,
y siempre el tronco de árbol a cuestas del titán.

"¡El Toqui, el Toqui!" clama la conmovida casta.
Anduvo, anduvo, anduvo. La Aurora dijo: "Basta,"
e irguióse la alta frente del gran Caupolicán.

Rubén Darío, *Azul* . . .

Caupolicán

Ya todos los caciques probaron el madero.
—¿Quién falta?—Y la respuesta fué un arrogante:—¡Yo!
—¡Yo!—dijo; y, en la forma de una visión de Homero,
del fondo de los bosques Caupolicán surgió.

Echóse el tronco encima, con ademán ligero;
y estremecerse pudo, pero doblarse no.
Bajo sus pies, tres días crujir hizo el sendero;
y estuvo andando . . . andando . . . y andando se durmió.

Andando, así, dormido, vió en sueños al verdugo:
él muerto sobre un tronco, su raza con el yugo,
inútil todo esfuerzo y el mundo siempre igual.

Por eso, al tercer día de andar por valle y sierra,
el tronco alzó en los aires y lo clavó en la tierra
¡como si el tronco fuese su mismo pedestal!

José Santos Chocano, *Alma América*

Speaking more generally, Chocano reflects many of the attitudes
of an age spirit of unrest and desire for broader horizons. Like all
the Modernists he is cosmopolitan. He has an inclination toward
paganism, but always within the boundaries of Christianity
(sentimental rather than theological). There is no preoccupation
with moral obligations in his work, with the possible exception of
Iras santas, nor with moral values. He possesses aristocratic
sentiments. If he had any democratic or social ideals in his youth,
he became convinced, like the others, that democracy would mean
the glorification of mediocrity.

On the other hand, Chocano's stubborn and virile optimism is the
antithesis of the prevailing despondency common among the poets
of his time, and stems from faith in himself. Morbidity is never
present in his work. Even in his youthful *En la aldea* the cemetery
is not a source of despair, but rather of wonder: "Why should this
mystery have the color of purity?" ("El Cementerio"). In "Morir,"
from the same collection, he speaks of his own death, defiantly,
indignantly: "To die young! A stupid calm which silences proud
songs." Doubt is the exception in his poetry. A faint sadness is
heard occasionally, but not until his last works does this tone
become anywhere near insistent.

Like all the Modernists, Chocano professed great admiration for
Walt Whitman, and his famous line "Walt Whitman tiene el
Norte; pero yo tengo el Sur" (Walt Whitman has the North; but I
have the South) seems to equate the two. But if Chocano felt little
kinship with the French writers, he had even less in common with
Whitman! On the surface, the Americanism of the two seems to
have the same breadth and scope, but what different Americas![17]
The arrogant Chocano sings of the glories of his personal Spanish
America: "I was Viceroy in the past, Captain of the conquests,
Monarch of the Sun; I was Yupanqui . . . I was Soto . . . I am Poet,
divine and sacred" ("Avatar"). This America is aristocratic or
savage. Whitman is the embodiment of a democratic America,
striving for future greatness. He is the poet of the multitudes, the
interpreter of the masses, and he identifies with the farmer, the

worker, the immigrant. We can no more imagine Chocano, the aristocrat, glorifying mechanics and pioneers than to envision Whitman, the fraternal, singing of viceroys and conquerors and an elegant colonial past! Contrast Whitman's democracy with Chocano's admiring dedication of *Alma América* to Alfonso XIII, or his alliance with dictators. Enormous stylistic differences separate them also. Whitman truly broke with traditional rhetoric; he was unconcerned about rhythm and rhyme or poetic responses. Chocano was not a stylistic reformer and limited himself for the most part to following tradition or the metrics of the Modernists. Nor is it possible to see much influence of the American poet in the work of Chocano. A few poems from the years 1908–17 show some Whitmanesque tinges, such as "Oda continental," which has a kind of Biblical meter often associated with Whitman. However, only "Oda salvaje," from that same period, has any real accent of Whitman, for here Chocano does occasionally sacrifice rhyme when necessary.

Edgar Allan Poe is the only other American writer who fascinated the Modernists. Poe's influence reached Spanish America for the most part through the indirect path of French inspiration.[18] Three or four of Chocano's compositions from the years 1908–14 reflect something from the poetry of Poe, chiefly "La campana de Dolores" (The Bell of Dolores):

> Las campanas
> del trineo
> que, livianas,
> van volcando en la blancura de las fúnebres sabanas
> el escándalo nervioso de su alegre tintineo;
> las campanas de las bodas
> que repican, como hablando de las cándidas promesas
> y de todas
> las dulzuras de los labios incitantes como fresas;

> Oh the bells
> of the sleigh,
> joyously
> spilling out in the white of the mournful plains,
> tingling sound all around of their happy clink;
> wedding bells,
> how they ring, how they sing of their candid vows,

and of all
that is sweet beckoning from the red, red lips.

P. R-P.

Among the Modernists Chocano is most closely allied with the
early Salvador Díaz Mirón,[19] whose stormy personal life so re-
sembled his own and whose intense, personal manner in his first
works affected Chocano greatly. The Mexican's youthful
"A Gloria" (proclaiming to his beloved that he was born like the
lion for combat) was quoted by all the Modernists, but it was
Chocano who fell visibly under this spell. In his first works Chocano
has something in common, also, with the active, optimistic spirit
of José Martí the man, not the poet.[20] He is the farthest apart from
Julio Herrera y Reissig, who took the opposite path of symbol and
suggestion and vagueness.

Chocano insistently styled himself a Parnassian after 1901. But
this poet was not a product of an intellectual culture which had
passed from an original Romanticism to the protective covering of
sculptured calmness in verse. Some of his sonnets do favor a
comparison with the polished sonnets of the French poet, José
María de Hérédia, as Chocano wished, chiefly because they are
descriptions of impersonal subjects. Yet even the exterior world—as
an example of the impersonal—becomes distinctly Chocanesque.
While nature remains apart from him in the sense that he does not
associate nature with his own states of soul, like the sentimental
Romantic, at the same time this exterior world becomes animated
in his hands. The mountains appear in attitudes of prayer, the river
swells up and protests, the twisted trees writhe in pain. It is true
that the descriptions are visual and Chocano does strive for
Parnassian objective beauty in his sonnets; yet he rarely loses his
forceful individualism which is apt to burst through even the
sonnets which come closest to Parnassian perfection. Therefore
there are critics who deny any Parnassian characteristics to
Chocano and who place him instead with the Romantics Espronceda, Byron, and Hugo. They profess to see nothing of Leconte de
Lisle or Hérédia, even in his propensity for the sonnet. In addition
to the intrusion of the personal, they point to the violence of his
images and the imbalance of his spirit—all far from the Parnassian
ideals.

Compare Darío's swan of chiseled and flawless cold beauty with Chocano's majestic condor. Even in his purely descriptive sonnet Chocano imparts a sense of pulsating power.

> El olímpico cisne de nieve
> con el ágata rosa del pico
> lustra el ala eucarística y breve
> que abre al sol como un casto abanico.
>
> De la forma de un brazo de lira
> y del asa de un ánfora griega
> es su cándido cuello, que inspira
> como prora ideal que navega.
>
> from "Blasón," *Prosas profanas*
> Rubén Darío

> Al despuntar el estrellado coro,
> pósase en una cúspide nevada:
> lo envuelve el día en la postrer mirada;
> y revienta á sus pies trueno sonoro.
>
> Su blanca gola es imperial decoro;
> su ceño varonil, pomo de espada;
> sus garfios siempre en actitud airada,
> curvos puñales de marfil con oro.
>
> from "El sueño del cóndor," *Alma América*
> José Santos Chocano

Symbolism offers endless variety instead of the narrower viewpoint of objective beauty as preached by the Parnassians. To stir an emotional response the Symbolist suggests, leaves vague impressions, invites the reader to give free rein to his own imagination. We have seen abundant evidence that Chocano purposely leaves little to the imagination of the reader. Vagueness, complexity of interpretation, and obscurity are not found in Chocano's poetry. There is no mysticism such as is encountered in Nervo. Chocano may have made occasional use of some of the esthetic aspects around the periphery of the symbol, but he does not take this as a definite course.

Many critics believe that Chocano appeared at too late a date in Latin American literature, when the intellectuals were already acquainted with the French writers Verlaine and Mallarmé, and they call him an unexpected throwback to the grandiloquence and overflowing passion of the Romantics. Even Chocano's most ardent admirers must admit that he is a poet of direct vision, one who shouts rather than suggests, and no one can deny the definite strokes of the Romantic in Chocano.

The poet's seemingly partial acceptance of Modernist artistic concepts, his apparent straddling of styles, accounts for the conflicting opinions of his critics as to the validity of his Modernism. It is obvious that Chocano possesses many salient characteristics of a formal Modernist poet. He is capable at times of creating a poem that falls in the center of Modernism, only to appear in other poems as a Romantic with but slight Modernist glints. Successive waves of Modernism sweep through his work submerging all else, and then recede without having toppled over the rock of his Romanticism. Chocano himself pointed to his descriptive sonnets as examples of his Parnassian objectivity, and occasionally he can indeed be classified a Parnassian for his polished expression; yet we have seen that even here he injects his own personality amid the flawless description. He has the objectivity of the epic poet; yet his individualism and his insistence on the ego come straight from the heart of a Romantic hero.

Is he, then, a Modernist? In the narrowest interpretation of formal Modernism, the combination of Parnassianism and Romanticism might in itself entitle him to be called a Modernist. In the broadest sense, his unity with the basic spirit of Modernism places him squarely in the ranks of the Modernists.

Chocano set out to cut a path between Whitman and Darío—to poeticize his grandiose visions of America with Modernist delicacy. In attempting to reconcile these two poles he wavered and sometimes stumbled, but the territory he claimed was his own.

As a major contributor to the development of Modernism, Chocano deserves his place among the great Modernists, and without apology. Even one of his harshest critics, who seems loath to group him with Darío, concludes by naming him one of the seven great Modernists of the movement (Anderson Imbert[21]).

In fact, Spanish American Modernism cannot be discussed without acknowledging the contribution of Chocano. Darío's leadership of the movement is unquestionable, but Chocano is always recognized as the initiator of *mundonovismo*. To Chocano alone belongs the honor of shifting the movement away from Paris toward America. Even if Chocano himself did not go beyond the threshold of the door he opened, he did point the way for future writers who in time would penetrate his descriptive America with their realistic social literature.

IV *The Fading of Modernism*

We might place the entire span of Modernism between the early 1880's and its evaporation during the years of World War I.[22] The most obvious reason for its diminishing influence was the force of contemporary events with their accompanying changes in circumstances and ideas. But it was the plethora of hackneyed imitators which really brought the movement into disrepute. Lacking exquisite poetic temperament and literary taste, they seized upon the most easily copied characteristics of the Modernists and made a mockery of artistry by their effeminate dilettantism and their unintelligible outpourings. The Spanish world soon became choked with the exaggeration of the Modernist esthetes who made a fetish of form and imagery and artificiality. The Mexican Revolution and World War I were scarcely conducive to exquisiteness even on the highest plane, and an intense reaction set in against the Modernist aristocratic exclusiveness.

Bejeweled and ornate Modernism, however, succeeded in bringing about an artistic revolution in the Spanish language, flowing for the first time from Spanish America to Spain. The source may have been French and cosmopolitan, but in its development it expressed the originality of a new people. The principal bequest to the literature was musical sound, and an enriched flexibility of form and rhythm. This youthful movement of a generation of Americans pressed the stamp of Hispano America on its work and opened the way for a more confident and mature expression of the authentic personality of Spanish America.

CHAPTER 5

The Later Poet

CHOCANO squandered his art amid incessant action during the
years following his hurried departure from Spain in 1908.
Politics, intrigues, revolutions filled his life as he flitted from the
government of one dictator or strong man to another. The compli-
mentary verses he offered in these host countries were often me-
diocre, but his audiences enjoyed the oratorical flare of his recitals.
Poems and articles were scattered throughout the presses of many
countries. Some poems were unpublished, in part because Chocano
withheld verses so as to have "new" material for his recitals upon
which he relied so heavily. His best poetry found its way into a few
collections which appeared from time to time.

I *Poetry from 1908 to 1920*

Chocano's publications from these years are disappointing. The
editions of 1908, 1912, and 1914 have a provisional aspect, as
though the poet had not quite finished with them. New poetry is
added in each book, but Chocano carried along much of the same
material from one to the other. There is beauty in these works, but
of a sort that promises rather than fulfills.

El Dorado: epopeya salvaje (The Golden Dream, 1908) was
published in Cuba and is actually "fragments of a book in preparation" according to the title page. The exuberant spirit and the
imagery mark the pieces as belonging to the years near *Alma
América*. Chocano himself is the hero of the first poem, "Prólogo
interior" (Interior Prologue), in which he proclaims: "America is
my only fountain of poetry . . ./That is why through my uninhibited
songs/twenty flags unfurl and twenty nations pass by,/one
hundred tyrants impose their will and one hundred revolutions
result." His concept of his place in American literature is clearly

stated: "I know that my fields await the sickle. Walt Whitman has the North; but I have the South."

Poemas escogidos (Selected Poems, 1912) is rarely discussed in Chocano's work because the book is made up of poetry already published or poetry that will appear again in better known collections, usually with numerous alterations. It is a singularly plain edition for Chocano, bare of prefaces or commentaries or even personal mottoes. There are six parts. The twenty-five poems of Part I come from *Alma América*, with no apparent reason for their choice other than having the celebrated "Los caballos de los conquistadores" as the opening poem. Part II, "Arte vida" (Art and Life), is made up of twenty-seven poems, of which eight come from the "Poemas modernistas" of *¡Fiat Lux!* and the rest belong to the years 1908–12. The poem "La gloria del proceso," which Chocano will use effectively during his 1925–27 imprisonment in Lima, appears here. Five compositions make up Part III entitled "Prosas líricas" (Lyric Prose), among these poems the well-known "Oda salvaje." Part IV, "De estampas newyorkinas" (From Prints of New York), contains four poems written in that city. Part V is a cluster of four "Nocturnos" which will reappear in final form with the entire set of "Nocturnos" in Volume IV of *Oro de Indias*. The sixth part is the poetry of *El Dorado*, with the subtitle "Savage Epic, in preparation." The "Prólogo interior" in this version omits five verses from the 1908 publication, including the famous line awarding the North to Whitman and the South to himself.

Puerto Rico lírico y otros poemas (probably 1914) is a slender book of poems published in San Juan. The prologue "El poeta de América" (The Poet of America), by the Puerto Rican poet Luis Llorens Torres, includes excerpts from a farewell speech which Chocano had given in the island in 1913.

The poetry is divided into four sections. Part I, with the heading "Puerto Rico lírico," contains fifteen new poems, beginning with "La ciudad encantada" (The Enchanted City), dedicated to San Juan. Some of the best compositions from these years are studded with fanciful imagery inspired by the Caribbean tropics and the sea. Part II, *El Dorado: epopeya salvaje*, uses the section from *Poemas escogidos* but places the ten poems in slightly different order and substitutes the poem "Oda salvaje" for "Noche salvaje" (Savage Night). The "Prólogo interior" follows the 1912 version. Part III, "Arte vida," has nine poems, four new works and five

from *Poemas escogidos* (including two originally from *¡Fiat Lux!*).
Part IV, "Estampas neoyorquinas," uses three poems from the
section in *Poemas escogidos*, omits one, and adds two new pieces.

Even though Chocano carried many of the poems from this
period into his final compilations, the poetry as it appears in these
collections is unequal to the triumphant work of *Alma América*
(1906) and *¡Fiat Lux!* (1908). This impression is heightened by a
comparison of the original with the final, polished versions of the
many poems Chocano included in *Primicias de oro de Indias* (1934),
as well as those he had worked on for *Oro de Indias* (1940, posthumously). It seems more appropriate, then, to discuss these poems
in their final setting.

The editions were limited and apparently not widely circulated,
for a number of critics writing in the 1920's, particularly Americans,[1] do not indicate any knowledge of these collections, especially
the last two.

Poesías selectas (A Selection of Poetry, no date) was published in
Paris, probably in 1920 or thereabouts, with a prologue by the
Peruvian writer, Ventura García Calderón. The collection is of
little importance, for it consists almost entirely of an odd assortment
of work from earlier collections. There are a few poems from *Iras
santas*, one from *En la aldea*, one from *El fin de Satán*, twenty-four
from *Alma América* (omitting some of the best known), two from
¡Fiat Lux!, one poem that had appeared in a Lima journal,[2] three
from *Poemas escogidos*, and one from *Puerto Rico lírico*. Four poems
appear which had not been seen in former collections: "Evocación"
(Evocation), "Prehistoria" (Prehistory), "Plegaria lírica" (A Lyric
Prayer), and "Oda continental."[3]

II   *Peruvian Years*

Chocano returned to Peru in 1921, in the aftermath of his
months as a political prisoner in Guatemala and his financial and
political shipwreck. The fervor of the "Coronation" scenes
acclaimed the poet the following year.

La coronación de José Santos Chocano (1924)[4] is an incredible
collection of coronation pieces which helps to explain both the
delusions of grandeur which persisted in Chocano's character
and the hatred which he provoked.

Pages of photographs of important Peruvian dignitaries confront
the reader at the outset, beginning with Señor don Augusto B.

Leguía, Constitutional President of the Republic, and ending with Chocano, wearing his crown of golden laurel leaves. More memorabilia follow, including greetings from the press (the powerful newspaper *El Comercio* is conspicuous by its absence), pictures of the speakers, cables received, and so on. The speeches in honor of Chocano are fascinating documents of the unbelievable adulation which resounded in the poet's ears. Chocano's own relatively short speech parallels portions of the words he had used in his farewell speech in Puerto Rico.[5]

Fourteen poems are included which Chocano recited at the "Fiesta of Poets" held in his honor during the evening ceremonies. Among these are new poems composed for the occasion and others which had not yet been published. "Plegaria lírica" opens the group, a poem to the Saint of Lima from the poet of Lima: "Between us we sum up the virtue of our race:/ecstasy and tumult, mysticism and clamor./Oh Patron Saint of the Americas, open your merciful mantle/for twenty nations to take refuge in your faith/. . . You may make them kneel down! But I want them standing!" The poem "En una casa colonial" (In a Colonial House) is a breath from the past which Chocano's talent, undiminished here, evokes so subtly and gracefully. Five "Nocturnos" appear, among the best of his work in this vein.[6] A section at the end, called "Post coronación," contains: three additional "Nocturnos," among them "El nocturno de la coronación" (The Coronation Nocturne), written in 1924; and "Tríptico de la torre" (Triptych of the Tower), three poems of 1914, 1919, and 1924. All the poetry from *La coronación* will reappear in Chocano's final works, in either *Primicias de oro de Indias* or *Oro de Indias*.

For years Chocano had dreamed of writing a vast American epic work. His *El Dorado* (insistently labeled "in preparation") was an attempt in this direction, but he never carried out his original design. As the poet frittered away his years embroiled in one turmoil after another, there was never time to undertake such an arduous task. Then in 1924 the opportunity came, but under rigid conditions of time and topic which Chocano accepted. To celebrate the centennial of the Battle of Ayacucho, the Peruvian government of Leguía assigned Chocano to compose a commemorative poem in honor of the date, December 9, 1924. In April of that year Chocano began his projected epic to be entitled *El Hombre-Sol, trazo de una epopeya panteísta* (The Sun-Man, a sketch of a pantheistic epic), of which he completed Canto IV, *Ayacucho y los Andes* (Ayacucho and the Andes), by November, 1924.

To compensate for Chocano's time and effort the government bought a certain number of copies in advance for the equivalent of about $35,000. Later the dictator Juan Vicente Gómez of Venezuela acquired another sizable amount, which fostered the gossip by the enemies of Leguía and the poet that Chocano had sold his inspiration.

Financially this was the most successful of Chocano's works, but esthetically it does not reach comparable heights. It is an involved, symbolic composition which depicts Bolívar as the savior of the Continent. While there are some passages of typical Chocanesque beauty, much of the exultant freshness and exuberance of earlier epic poems is lacking. A diminished power shows through the elaborate sonority.

Chocano begins with an explanation of each of the cantos that he intends to compose for the entire epic. The prose description relates that Simón Bolívar, evoking the ruins of Rome, has sworn to liberate the Sun which has been chained for three centuries to the foot of the throne of Carlos V. The Sun sends his spirit to Bolívar in the afternoon's last ray, and thus Bolívar is transfigured into the *Hombre-Sol*, the Sun-Man. The shade of the heroic Inca Túpac-Amaru hands him a sword of fire, and the *Hombre-Sol* leaves for America.

Canto IV, *Ayachucho y los Andes*, is the only one completed in verse.[7] In the poetry the Andes awaken from a deep sleep, and as they stretch, the snow drops in pieces and cracks appear in the stone. Calling to one another, they announce that they see the Sun made man, the beloved Son who wishes to see his Father loosened from his chains. All the peaks burst into a hosanna of exultation. From their heights they look down on the struggle of two armies, and they salute the heroes whose restless swords are sparkling in the sun. From peak to peak they call out what they see, the names of the heroes, their banners. Out of the terrible clash the *Hombre-Sol* appears victorious.

In the final section of the poem, the hero directs his words to the obscure voices of nature. He has fulfilled his promises. His sword can be thrust into the crest of Condorcunca, which from this day will be the sacred mountain peak of America. The sword will become a flaming cross, growing with the centuries. The peaks break the silence they have kept in his presence and proclaim that the sun of Carlos V has begun to set. Their hymn is joyous, for the father Sun is free. Night falls and the *Hombre-Sol* dreams. After fourteen years he awakens. His work is beautiful and he understands that in America the Sacred Empire of nature has begun.

At the end of Canto IV, Chocano places a running commentary in prose where he fills in the details of the battles, the locations, names, and the like, and explains references to Christ, Prometheus, and others. A concluding paragraph states that the sense of nature always predominated in Bolívar and around this axis whirls the pantheistic spirit of the entire epic.

President Leguía wrote a short prologue in the form of a letter, dated October 14, 1924. He addresses Chocano as "Poet Laureate" and voices his belief that this Epic of the Liberator will inspire a continental spirit and contribute to the eventual unity of America! Leguía placed his sights too high. The composition did achieve a contemporary success, but chiefly because it was hailed by the ever-present supporters of the poet who were still faithful to his poetic voice. Time, however, has not sustained their verdict.

This epic is very different from the stirring, exultant *La epopeya del Morro*, and even further removed from the blazing indignation of Chocano's youthful *Iras santas* of epic spirit, which had seemed to rail against social injustice. In *Ayacucho y los Andes* the dialogue of the peaks holds beauty and strength, and there is originality in the concept of beholding the battle through their eyes. Nevertheless, there is a tiresome, heavy quality throughout the long, elaborate composition. Those waiting expectantly for another major work as promised in the "works in progress," 1906, must have felt a vague disappointment, even if they did not admit it to themselves.

The poet was forty-nine. *Ayacucho y los Andes* was the last epic poem that Chocano undertook. Even though far from his best, it might have opened up new possibilities for his epic art. Instead, the tragic event of the next year turned Chocano into another path, directing him first to his prose *El libro de mi proceso* and then on to the earnest intimacy of his new "Nocturnos" and the other sensitive personal pieces of his last poetry.

III   *Chocano's Prose*[8]

It seems appropriate at this point to comment briefly on the prose of Chocano, even though the prose writer is so inferior to the poet. The style is intense and complicated and is always oratorical with large doses of arrogance. Actually, the importance of Chocano's prose does not lie with its literary value, but with the dramatic effects on his own life.

In general his prose writings served to explain himself or his dogmatic political doctrines, and frequently they involved the author in heated controversies. *Idearium tropical*[9] (Lima, 1922)—containing his views on well-organized dictatorships as opposed to the farce of democracy—led to an acrimonious involvement in Peruvian politics. *El libro de mi proceso* (Lima, 1927–28), which eventually grew out of this controversy, is a three-volume, eight-hundred-page tome (including a few poems) in which Chocano attempted to explain his lack of guilt in the encounter with Elmore. He also sought to justify his life and restate his most controversial political views. The title page alone, with its reference to the "exploitation of the cadaver of Elmore for the benefit of Bolshevik snobbism outside Peru, and within, for the plutocratic oligarchy," illustrates the tone of the pages that follow. The work is flagrantly defensive at times, abusively aggressive and unrepentant at other times. From a literary standpoint, it is involved and unpolished. Like all Chocano's prose, it provided his enemies with additional ammunition to hurl against him, and he became completely discredited in the eyes of the liberals throughout the Continent.

Chocano's most important prose work is *Memorias. Las mil y una aventuras* (Memoirs. The Thousand and One Adventures, 1940, posthumously), an autobiography from the material which the author had published in newspapers and magazines of the Continent during 1930–31. Chocano pictures himself as a dashing, Byronic hero, a knight in shining armor saving the peace of the Continent or organizing the government of his country. ("How I Averted a War in Central America and Organized a Government in Perú" is his modest heading for Chapter 19.)

As Chocano was having financial difficulties when he wrote these *Memorias*, he tried to put forth details which would interest his reading public. The description of his childhood during the War of the Pacific is very vivid, an ironical twist in a way because he was writing in Chile. His comments about contemporary writers whom he has known hold a fascination. In general, the lesser known poets come out very well, but Rubén Darío receives innumerable verbal thrusts, and it is obvious that even in 1931 Chocano could not abide his gigantic literary reputation. Among the many Spanish writers whom he discusses, the author singles out Pérez Galdós for his kindest remarks, but states his dislike of the cold Echegaray.

The *Memorias* deal with years that held great glory and acclaim for Chocano, and they stop abruptly in 1907, just short of the dark periods in his life. Undoubtedly this contributes to an over-all disappointment, for the work lacks the intimate, soul-searching note that sets an autobiography apart from other literary genres.

In the final analysis, Chocano resorted to prose only to narrate what was important for him, to attack, or to defend himself. Nevertheless, it is clear from his writings that he was a man of his time, completely entangled in contemporary events. From his prose we glean more explicit opinions, but none is contrary to what he wrote in his infinitely superior poetry.[10]

IV *Chilean Epilogue*

Turning his back on Lima, scene of his greatest triumphs and his recent crushing dishonor, Chocano elected to make his home in Santiago de Chile. During those last years he tried valiantly to remake his life and to polish his art.[11]

The great impulse of that closing period was a vast collection of past work, together with new poetry, which Chocano intended to entitle *Oro de Indias: poemas neo-mundiales*. In 1934, the poet decided to publish *Primicias de oro de Indias*, the "first fruits" of this endeavor. Happily this book—his final personal publication—restored some of the luster once attached to his name.

In a brief preface Chocano explains that *Oro de Indias* will be a collection of poetry in nine parts. At random he has gathered representative selections from each of these to form two volumes of *Primicias de oro de Indias*. (Actually there was time to complete only one volume, with poems from the first four parts.[12]) The poet states that all his poems are suggested by either the nature or the history of America—discounting the universality of the themes in the section "Fantasía errante" (Errant Fantasy)—or by his own life, lived under the only indispensable law of poetry which is that of sincerity. To close these preliminary and, for Chocano, unelaborate remarks, he adds his two well-known mottoes, a gesture borrowed from his youth which contrasts strangely with the explanatory tone of the rest.

Almost as if he felt it necessary to reaffirm his position in American literature, Chocano displays words of the future Nobel Laureate, Gabriela Mistral, on the next page—"To José Santos Chocano, to the Peruvian and to the poet of the Continent, Teacher of all"—along with excerpts from the laudatory opinions of two critics, George Umphrey and Max Daireaux. Far away are the days when Chocano published in red or blue print. He had neither the power to command a press nor the necessary disposition. Even over the years we have a clear picture of this proud figure— once so lionized, now so fallen in public opinion—reasserting his right to be heard.

Given the haphazard and hasty, unpolished manner in which Chocano had published his work after 1908, much of his poetry through these years had been seen by only a limited reading public. A poet of such rich imagination, such color and emotion, would have an enormous amount of material to exhibit. *Primicias de oro de Indias* is culled from poetry written as far back as 1908 on up to poems composed precisely for inclusion in this collection. Chocano himself gives no indication of previous publication dates, perhaps in part because he was reworking so much of the original. Careful checking reveals that many of the poems had been published in various journals and newspapers of Central and South America during the years 1908-18. Six poems come from *El Dorado* (1908), ten from *Poemas escogidos* (1912), ten from *Puerto Rico lírico* (1914?), two from *Poesías selectas* (1920?)—all with attendant changes. A few were written in 1920 during his imprisonment in Guatemala. Some the poet had recited in Lima in 1922, also included in the volume *La coronación de José Santos Chocano* (1924). Still others come from *El libro de mi proceso* (1927-28). Throughout the poetry numerous lines and stanzas are suppressed or rewritten, titles are changed, in some cases there is even a complete revision of the first version (for example "El baño de los caballos" [The Splashing Horses], originally from *El Dorado*, and "Por los canales" [Through the Canals], from *Puerto Rico lírico*). Twelve love poems to Margarita, written from 1921-25, appear for the first time in *Primicias*, and will be published again posthumously by Chocano's widow. A few of the finest compositions come from the years 1931-34.

Thus *Primicias de oro de Indias* is a book of various epochs in the poet's life and a sampling of many different facets of his art.

Although we still hear the sounds of the earlier Chocano, there is a distinct tone to this collection, a riper, perfected tone with less intensity and blaze. The stridently impossible has been shaded. There is often disenchantment in the treasure chest.

In "Profesión de fe" (Profession of Faith)[13] Chocano says: "And the dialogue between God and me begins: 'Did you produce goodness?' 'Not always, but Beauty, yes'." Certain poems speak of the entwining of his life and his poetry: "Espaldarazo" (Accolade) and "Orgullo" (Pride)[14]—"I have the pride and the sadness of living a poem and writing it afterwards." "Vida errabunda" (The Life of a Wanderer) includes nine poems dedicated to cities of America which have inspired him. "Ciudad blanca" (White City), a vision of Arequipa, and "Ciudad olvidada" (Forgotten City), a corner of the Andes, belong to Peru.

The magnificence of earlier periods is still present. Some of the poetry possesses the rich, glittering qualities of the 1906–08 period. "Cumbre y río" (Peak and River), for example, is as full of imaginative Chocanesque figures as any poem in *Alma América;* (The snow on the peak seems like a sheep's twisted fleece, from which a river breaks forth in zigzag form, as a skein unravels):

> La nieve de la cúspide semeja
> el vellón retorcido de una oveja
> del que, haciendo un zig-zag a su albedrío
> se va, ágilmente, desprendiendo un río,
> como se desenvuelve una madeja.

In "El baño de los caballos" the descendants of the conquerors' steeds snort and splash in a sparkling river. This poem, completely reworked for *Primicias,*[15] has all the dash and forceful excitement of similar pieces written at the peak of his career. Brilliant, fanciful imagery stands out in other poems; (Bands of green butterflies swirl over the beds of fine emeralds. Green wings decorated with dust from the mines? Or are the butterflies fluttering stones? "Esmeraldas y mariposas" [Emeralds and Butterflies][16]):

> Sobre el criadero de esmeraldas finas,
> verdes mariposas giran en bandadas:
> ¿polvo de alas verdes cuájase en las minas
> o las mariposas son piedras aladas?

In "Los toros pasan"[17] Chocano displays his rhythmic, verbal art. The "Dedicatoria" (Dedication) to the memory of his glorious ancestor, the Great Captain Don Gonzalo de Córdoba, brings a wave of nostalgia for a proud past. The lovely "Las Vicuñas" (The Vicuñas), with overtones of Chocano's Modernism, is a delicate, graceful composition:

> Vicuñas fugitivas de alada ligereza
> hacia la nieve corren a reflejar sus sombras,
> como si las guiaran instintos de pureza
> y sus pies delicados reclamaran alfombras.
> . . . .
> Tal son por signo heráldico, hechas a las alturas,
> a las melancolías y a las serenidades:
> aman las cumbres frías, aman las nieves puras,
> aman las lejanías, aman las soledades.
> . . . .
> Pulidas y sedeñas, románticas y leves,
> en un galope lleno de agilidad y gracia,
> huyendo hacia el reposo de las perpetuas nieves,
> refugian en las cumbres su esquiva aristocracia.

> Elusive vicuñas with the swiftness of wings,
> run toward the snow where shifting form and shadow meet,
> as if instincts were guiding their steps toward pure things,
> and carpets were needed for their delicate feet.
> . . . .
> By heraldic design, they are destined for heights,
> melancholy quiet and deep serenity.
> They love the cold peaks, they love solitary sites.
> They love the pure snows, and they love tranquillity.
> . . . .
> Polished and silken, romantic figures aglow,
> with springing leaps full of agility and grace,
> fleeing to the repose of perpetual snow,
> their shy aristocracy seeks the highest place.
>
> *P. R-P.*

Sometimes Chocano is admirable in adversity, and certain poems which he wrote in prison convey a sense of his dauntless spirit. He includes a group from the penitentiary in Guatemala—when he was under sentence of death—in which he speaks of the liberty that has fled, the health that has left him, the hatred surrounding him, and the consolation he receives from being able to respond with a poem. "Elegía epicúrea" (An Epicurean Elegy), another composition probably written at the same time, is dedicated to a fellow poet but certainly applies to himself. There is the bravado we expect from Chocano, but he also has the grace to admit that where life has been enjoyed to the hilt, certain consequences must be accepted: "A useless life? I only know that it was beautiful."

By contrast "Serenamente" (Serenely),[18] written during his prison days in Lima, is full of bitterness and belligerence. "So many have slandered me/and have jeered at me/and have given such magnitude to my sin/that it grieves me not to have committed it." "La orgullosa piedad" (Piety with Pride),[19] directed to his sister, has the same biting tone. Sneering at his adversaries he asks her to pray for those who have caused him to suffer—but not from piety, rather because they have contributed to his greatness and superiority!

We often catch glimpses of a battered soul looking for interior peace, which drives the poet to say that he longs for solitude. "I want to enclose myself in a crystal tower, in front of the assault of the waves—but alone" ("Extasis" [Ecstasy]). Another personal, but not flamboyant, note is struck in "No me despertéis" (Do not awaken me),[20] where he speaks of the deep satisfaction of being the sole owner of an idea, a dream, a grief, anything—and in hiding it so that no one else knows. "¿Dónde estoy?" (Where am I?) is reminiscent of some of the poems of personal regret found in *¡Fiat Lux!*: "I have gone astray and I do not find myself. What road have I taken?" "La vida náufraga" (The Shipwrecked Life)[21] tells us that he seeks a plot of earth in which to plant a rose bush since men will not let him build a high tower. But "instead of the tree that takes root, I am scarcely a log condemned to the convulsive insomnia of the sea." He knows that at his death he will finally have his plot of ground where they will bury him as he wishes, *in a standing position!*

Deeply moving is his sincere and beautiful "Elegía marcial" (A Martial Elegy), written in Guatemala, in 1909, in memory of the recent death of his father: "The death of my father has saddened my soul. . . . Oh Father, I will never have your happiness. I will always live for the stadium, and you knew how to live for the home. Father, you did not know the horror of popularity, nor were you crowned with the thorns of envy. You have lived without tumult and you have died in peace."

Matching this poem in sincerity, but much more tragic in tone, is "Elegía hogareña," written in 1931 or 1932 after the death of his mother. Trembling with choked sobs, the poet speaks of his home struck down by death. The images shift and change in the half-light. Everything recalls the goodness of this gentle woman. Even the furniture mourns for the absent mother who has left her imperishable remembrance in the depths of his solitude. "After the death of my mother the old house where I lived only yesterday seems like a cemetery to me, in which the inanimate pieces of furniture are cadavers. . . . I fall to my knees asking: Mother! Oh Mother! Where are you?" In his suffering the poet does not renounce his past laurels, but his humility in the presence of his anguish clothes them with dignity.

The poems of his last years are those of a poet who has come to terms with life. He knows these are his closing years, and with dignity and a calm pride—ever retaining his inherent and individual characteristics—he allows himself to be carried along by the inevitable tides of time.

"Tesoro oculto" (1932 or 1933) praises all the hidden treasures of which he has dreamed, and even indicates the fever that led him to dig for buried treasure in Chile. But he concludes: "If I do not find the gold . . . pride will remain, together with the enchantment of having lived a story from the Thousand and One Nights."

"Finigénito" (1934), probably his last poem, is filled with loving tenderness. Looking at his seven-year-old son, the poet remembers the painful glory of his own life, the triumphs and the defeats. All is reflected and purified in this child who is so much a part of his own spirit. Chocano is at last a father who loves his son more than himself:

Hijo mío: en tus ojos se refleja mi vida.
. . . .
Resucito en ti . . . Sólo se explica así el cariño
de que por ti estoy lleno más que por mí. Daría
mi dolor de hombre en pago de tu placer de niño.

Sin dejar de ser ángel, comienzas ya a ser hombre.
¿No te quiebra las alas el peso de mi nombre?
Como purificado quedo con tu pureza,
la vida en mí concluye por ser la que en ti empieza.

My son: my entire life is reflected in your eyes.

. . . .

I am resurrected in you. How else can I explain
this immense love for you which overwhelms me. I would give
my grief as a man to pay for your pleasure as a child.

Without ceasing to be an angel, you are becoming
a man. Will not the weight of my name break your angel wings?
As though purified I now exist with your purity.
Life in me concludes by being that which begins in you.

P. R-P.

Until the publication of *Primicias de oro de Indias* in 1934, there
had been nothing to rival the poet's outstanding work of 1906 and
1908. Only three books of any consequence had appeared during
this extended span of years: *Poemas escogidos* (1912) and *Puerto
Rico lírico* (1914?), both of somewhat unfinished aspect; and
Ayacucho y los Andes (1924), entirely epic and lacking in the
vitality of his earlier poetry. *Primicias,* therefore, represents
Chocano's maximum effort—his mature, polished art. Many of the
compositions have deepened into true lyricism, causing us to forget
the tinseled baubles of his earlier work. Indeed these new notes
from his loneliness and self-imposed exile offer a poignant balance
to the cloak-and-dagger hero of earlier days.

Primicias was meant to be just a sample of his great compilation
Oro de Indias, but it became, instead, his last personal effort. While
the work did not achieve the international fame of *Alma América,*
it did revive much of Chocano's literary reputation, except in his
own country.

V   Posthumous Poetry

Poemas del amor doliente (Poems of a Suffering Love, 1937) is the
first of the posthumous works sanctioned by Chocano's widow. It is
a collection of intimate love poems written to her by the poet
during their secret courtship of the years 1921–24 and the early
days of their marriage.[22] Chocano was approaching fifty at that
time, and Margarita was twenty-one. Deep emotion runs through
all the work, made somehow more moving by the romanticism of
the mature poet before this youthful, final love. The sincerity,
a concern for her, and his need so openly expressed reveal unexpected qualities in Chocano, particularly when contrasted with

the boasting so evident in the affected love poems of the early *Azahares*.

The poet seems to have laid aside his complications and his arrogance in the tenderness of this love, thus uncovering recesses carefully hidden until this time: "Seated very close to me, you place a hand of tenderness on my head, now gray, and miraculously it becomes dark once more" ("Nocturno angustiado de las últimas reminiscencias" [An Anguished Nocturne of Last Memories]). His passionate obsession with her voice, her eyes, her mouth, her little feet seems that of a young, ecstatic lover: "I would put my hands like sandals on your bare feet, and tie them with the knot of a kiss so that you would never loosen them" ("Elogio de los pies" [In Praise of Your Tiny Feet]). Sometimes he treats her like a little child: "My beautiful little porcelain doll" ("Poupee" [Little Doll]). A few poems have a playful, coy tone: "El gato bandido" (The Sly Cat), "La plegaria del lobo" (The Wolf's Prayer), "El lobo enamorado" (The Enamored Wolf)—"Take pity on your wolf, little Red Riding Hood. Oh! How very late I found you in my path."

Other poems allow lyric glimpses of their moments together, their dreams, their walks oblivious of those around them. He speaks of the son he longs for. In a humble tone he writes: "And our union seems so perfect that God will scarcely note the soldering" ("Nocturno de la incineración" [Nocturne of Incineration]).

But a separation occurred, which corresponds to a time when Chocano was alone in Lima. "Nocturno de la separación" (Nocturne of Separation) reveals the intensity of his autumnal love and his anguish at her absence: "It is the first night without you. Your pillow next to mine has a funereal aspect. . . . I take your flowers to accompany me, shedding their leaves over your pillow case at my side. Thus when morning comes, I will have a handful of roses clasped next to my heart."

Of the twenty-four poems in *Amor doliente* twelve had been included by Chocano in his *Primicias* (1934), and one in *La Coronación* (1924). Evidently the poet did not consider the rest as mature for publication, in spite of the lyric force of many, or he felt that they were too personal. His widow published them all with pride.

Chocano was not given the time to finish his projected *Oro de Indias* personally. However, the material he was working on appeared posthumously in four volumes under the general title he had chosen. *Oro de Indias* consists of Vol. I, "Pompas solares," 1939; Vol. II, "Fantasía errante," 1940; Vol. III, "Sangre incaica, Estampas newyorkinas y madrileñas," 1941; Vol. IV, "Nocturnos intensos, Las mil y una noches de América," 1941. (The Gold of the Indies. Vol. I, Sun-drenched Pageantry; Vol. II, Errant Fantasy; Vol. III, Incaic Blood, Prints of New York and Madrid; Vol. IV, Ardent Nocturnes, The Thousand and One Nights of America.)

Primicias showed evidence of careful artistry and demonstrated the high standards which the poet had set for himself. *Oro de Indias* does not have the benefit of these personal finishing touches. Chocano left notes, sketches, and indications for grouping, showing his intention to revise and rework the poetry planned for this compilation; but it was almost inevitable that certain provisional overtones could not be erased from such a collection. The careless editing, however, is inexcusable.[23] And because confidence in the editors is severely shaken by glaring errors, we do not know whether certain striking changes from the original poetry are to be attributed to Chocano or to editorial whim.[24]

Yet in spite of all that is disconcerting, these volumes offer some of Chocano's finest work. As in *Primicias* the poetry displays many facets of his art. We behold again the panoramic beauty of America, the poet's dreams of Continentalism, and his rich, imaginative evocations of the past; but new and unexpected lights shine out from time to time. The general tone of the collection is that of *Primicias*, less blazing and exuberant than his youthful work, more in accord with the calm pride of a man who has not won all the battles of life.

Chocano's well-known "Prólogo lírico" (its final title) opens the volumes, appearing again with the original 1908 lines. "Oda salvaje,"[25] of the same epoch, is bursting with love for America, savage and beautiful in Chocano's eyes. Apparently written during the voyage back to her shores after a bitter experience in Spain, the poet rejoices in the Continent's magnificence and strength, and in the role he attributes to himself: "I know that the centuries have singled me out as your Poet." "Oda continental"[26] reflects not only the beauty of America but Chocano's continued ideal of continental unity: "On the shores of memory I listen to the murmur of our future glories." He has watched the procession of ancient Emperors, Conquerors, and Viceroys; now he hears the solemn, slow steps of twenty Republics advancing. "Twenty? Puerto Rico knows . . . that even the Olympic eagle cannot be merciless with the paschal lamb." And thus twenty flags unfurl in the poet's dreams, "like a prism that refracts a great rainbow from the Andes, spreading over the twenty Republics." These two poems, "Oda salvaje" and "Oda continental," have often been linked with Whitman's work, in both scope and style. Actually one must strain to find the so-called Whitmanesque swing in this poetry, since the flavor of Chocano is so evident.

Other poems from this same period deal with topics outside Chocano's usual sphere. "La muerte del aviador"[27] is dedicated to Jorge Chávez, Peruvian flier who was the first to cross the Alps and whom Chocano calls "the quixotic symbol of our nervous age." "The monoplane lies in pieces before the hero. It has fallen in Icarian stubbornness, but a breath of wind or of delirium still makes the wings stir from time to time." The poem "La elegía del 'Titanic' " (probably 1914) marks Chocano as a poet of his era. Strikingly vivid are the groping, grasping hands, flaying the water in their anguished search for help. "Oda cíclica" (A Cyclic Ode)[28] and "Suprema pax" (Supreme Peace), while not of the same level of artistry, show Chocano's involvement in the catastrophe of World War I.

Several poems come from Chocano's Mexican years. "Proclama lírica" (A Lyric Proclamation, 1915) speaks of the glowing inspiration of the Mexican Revolution in spite of an unknown outcome: "Resplendent, tormented Mexico. . . . What does it matter that you have plowed in the sea, or I have written in the sands?" "Himno marcial" (A Martial Hymn) is dedicated to the young heroes of Chapultepec and calls for unity among the twenty nations. Other poems illustrate the poet's personal involvement in the Mexican Revolution, as "Sinfonía heroica" (A Heroic Symphony, 1913), dedicated to the assassinated President Madero and Vice-President Pino Suárez, and "Ultima rebelión," written from Guatemala around 1920 and dedicated to Villa. "Oda cívica" (A Civic Ode)[29] was read in Guatemala at the inauguration of a monument to Benito Juárez and voices hopes for future continental greatness when nations grouped together will form a cordillera as strong as the Andes. "La campana de Dolores," written in 1914 or 1915 and clearly built on Poe's composition "The Bells," praises the Mexican bell with the most complete soul, the one which swings like a cradle—the redemptive bell ringing for freedom.

There are several poems originally from *Puerto Rico lírico* (1914?), with the rigorous changes and revisions begun in *Primicias*. ("Tarde antillana" [Antillean Afternoon], for example, is completely different from the original.) "La última visión" (The Last Vision, 1916), dedicated to the memory of Rubén Darío, is the expected tribute. Much better are the crystalline notes of "La flauta encantada" (The Enchanted Flute), a short poem written in Costa Rica in 1921 on the fifth anniversary of Darío's death. The varied poems of these periods in Chocano's life are grouped together in the first two volumes.[30]

"Estampas madrileñas" (Prints of Madrid), part of Volume III, contains Chocano's Spanish pieces, among them the bitter "La leyenda negra (Fin de raza)" (The Black Legend; Death of a Race, 1908), beginning: "Legendary race, museum-piece country, Spain is like a macabre vision."[31] This is followed by "La leyenda áurea (Fe de raza)" (The Golden Legend; Faith of a Race), written sometime after 1910, which more than compensates for the first: "Joyful race, golden country of the sun, Spain is like a radiant vision."

"Estampas newyorkinas," in the same volume, exhibits his impressions of New York. Like many Latin American poets, Chocano feels uneasy in this environment, which causes him to utter disparaging phrases: "There is nothing that oppresses my heart as much as a country sick with civilization"; "A city is not worth more than a rose garden"; "But Lord, where are the fluttering wings of poetry?" ("Ciudad fuerte" [The Strong City]). A prayer in St. Patrick's Cathedral, "Oración sencilla" (A Simple Prayer), probably 1908, approximates a tone of humility, still an impossible feat for the Chocano of that era.

Much of the poetry from the section "Sangre incaica" will remain among the poet's lasting contributions. The first four poems (often called "Notes of the Indigenous Soul") are a surprising departure from the disdainful and arrogant Chocano of old:

"Otra vez será" (Perhaps Another Time)[32] gives the enigmatic answer of a young Indian to the misfortunes that beset him. "Oh haughty and scornful race under the appearances of humility.

Never defeat nor anger nor fear change one muscle in your facial
expression. . . . No grief, no catastrophe is capable of taking away
your virile serenity. . . . The Race waits, waits, waits. It spins and
spins without ceasing."

"¡Quién sabe!" (Who knows?) has become one of Chocano's
most quoted poems:

> Indio que labras con fatiga
> tierras que de otros dueños son,
> ¿ignoras tú que deben tuyas
> ser, por tu sangre y tu sudor?
> ¿ignoras tú que audaz codicia
> siglos atrás, te las quitó?
> ¿ignoras tú que eres el amo?
>   —¡Quién sabe, señor!
>
> Indio de frente taciturna
> y de pupilas sin fulgor,
> ¿qué pensamiento es el que escondes
> en tu enigmática expresión?
> ¿Qué es lo que sueña tu silencio?
> ¿Qué es lo que oculta tu dolor?
> ¿Qué es lo que buscas en tu vida?
> ¿Qué es lo que imploras a tu Dios?
>   —¡Quién sabe, señor!
>
> . . . .
>
> ¡Oh, raza antigua y misteriosa
> de impenetrable corazón,
> que sin gozar ves la alegría
> y sin sufrir ves el dolor:
> eres augusta como el Ande,
> El Grande Océano y el Sol!
> Ese tu gesto que parece
> como de vil resignación,
> es de una sabia indiferencia
> y de un orgullo sin rencor.
>
>
> "Oh Indian, with weariness,
> for other owners do you toil.
> Don't you know your blood and sweat
> give you title to the soil?
> Don't you know that ancient greed

came to rob you and despoil?
Don't you know that you are master?"
        "Who knows, señor!"

"Oh Indian with somber brow,
what thoughts are those you hide
behind that enigmatic look
of eyes where hope has died?
What does your silence mean?
What grief is at your core?
What do you seek in life,
and from your God implore?"
            "Who knows, señor!"

. . . .
    Oh ancient and mysterious race
of impenetrable heart,
You see joy without enjoyment,
and from grief remain apart.
You are august like the Andes,
like the Sun and the great Sea.
Your expression, while appearing
that of base servility,
is one of wise indifference
and pride without hostility.

P. R-P.

"Ahí, no más" (Just Over There) is the Indian's impassive reply
to the traveler, no matter how far away his destination. The poet
asks, "And where is the city?" "Just over there." He crosses one
peak after another, but still each Indian repeats, "Just over there."
To Chocano this monotonous answer expresses the scorn of a wise
race toward the ironies of distant goals. Possessing the same
ancestral title, he will also say "just over there" when they question
him about where he is going in pursuit of his dreams.

"¡Así será!" (So Be It) pictures in blinding clarity the abject
misery of the Indian, caught in the net of his tragic circumstances:

Clarín de guerra pide sangre.
Truena la voz del Capitán:
—Indio: ¡a las filas! Blande tu arma
hasta morir o hasta triunfar.
Tras la batalla, si es que mueres,
nadie de ti se acordará:

pero sí, en cambio, el triunfo alcanzas,
te haré en mis tierras trabajar.
No me preguntes por qué luchas,
ni me preguntes dónde vas—
Dócil el indio entra en las filas
como un autómata marcial;
y sólo dice, gravemente:
                              —Así será.

. . . .

¿Resignación? Antes orgullo
de quien se siente valer más
que la fortuna caprichosa
y que la humana crueldad.

Un filosófico desprecio
hacia el dolor acaso da
la herencia indígena a mi sangre,
pronto a fluir sin protestar;
y cada vez que la torpeza
de la Fortuna huye a mi afán,
y crueldades harto humanas
niéganle el paso a mi Ideal,
y hasta la Vida me asegura
que nada tengo que esperar,
dueño yo siempre de mí mismo
y superior al bien y al mal,
digo, encogiéndome de hombros:
                              —Así será.

The trumpet of war calls for blood.
The voice of the Captain thunders:
"Fall into line, Indian, wield your sword
either for death or for triumph.
After the battle, if you die,
there will be none to think of you.
But if, instead, you're victorious,
I will make you toil on my lands.
Do not ask the reason you fight,
nor in what direction you go."
Docile, the Indian takes his place
like a robot destined for war;
and only says, gravely, the words:
                              "So be it."

. . . .
Resignation? No. It is pride
of one who believes he's worth more
than the whims of capricious fate
or the cruelty of mankind.

A philosophic scorn toward pain
perhaps is my inheritance
ancestral, flowing in my blood
so quick to spill without protest;
time and again my eagerness
is thwarted by dull Fortune's ban,
and cruelties of human hand
deny my steps toward an Ideal,
and even Life itself insists
that I can hope for nothing here.
Yet I am master of my soul,
superior to good and ill.
I shrug my shoulders and repeat:
      "So be it."

               P. R-P.

In these four poems there is an undeniable awareness of the pitiful conditions of the Indian, a scorned and rejected outcast in his country. The youthful aristocrat of Lima would not have deigned to notice, but life's disappointments and defeats chastened this soul. "Otra vez será" had been praised when the poet recited it at his "Coronation" in 1922. However, Chocano's own generation had no sustained interest in this aspect of his poetry, and the younger generation arrived at such a dislike and distrust of Chocano that they could not credit him with any sincerity. The new writers, especially those aligned with Nativism and Social Poetry, were in fact incensed at Chocano's acceptance of the Indian's position, the lauding of his serenity, the lack of suggestion for social change, and the inevitable, unrealistic personal lesson drawn at the end. Foreign opinion, on the other hand, places these four poems among the finest of Chocano's work.

Other poetry from "Sangre incaica" draws from the well of evocations of a great Inca past. "Ante una vasija incaica" (Before an Incaic Vessel), for example, which was also recited at the "Coronation," is as haunting and nostalgic as the much earlier "Momia incaica" of *Alma América*.

The "Nocturnos" of Volume IV are among the most lyric and most personal of Chocano's poems, gathered from 1908 to 1920, and from 1921 to 1928 in "De mis nuevos nocturnos" (From My New Nocturnes). In this work the poet has freed himself from his sword-brandishing, oratorical style, and there is a simplicity and clarity which speaks to the heart.

The tender and emotional "Nocturno del regreso al hogar" (Nocturne of My Homecoming)[33] is filled with the sweetness of his return to his mother's home after twenty years of wandering: "This first night in my mother's home revives my soul. . . . I have lived a poem, and Mother I am exhausted. . . . The smoke of glory asphyxiates me. I long for a tranquil corner in which to live." "Nocturno del viaje" (Nocturne of the Journey)[34] is a poignant description of those twenty years: "Mother, I have traveled far. I have traveled constantly. I am weary, but I do not repent of the path I have traveled." Disillusion is more often his companion now than resounding defiance. In return, he has a certain wisdom and self-understanding. The final version of "Nocturno del viaje" in *Oro de Indias* suppresses the last twenty-seven lines found in *La Coronación* (1924) and *Primicias* (1934). Instead, these lines appear at the end of "El nocturno de la nueva despedida" (Nocturne of the New Farewell).[35] Particularly expressive are his concluding verses; (I went in search of myself, and today I return. I have found myself at last. A child again? A child for my mother. Her kiss tells me so. . . . My childhood was somber. . . . Is anyone a child without play and laughter? As I never possessed a childhood, I know that I have never ceased being a child. So I come to tell you, Mother . . . that I have found myself here, as if I had never been separated from you):

> Me fuí a viajar en busca de mí; y hoy que regreso,
> llego a encontrarme. Encuéntrome, al fin . . . ¿Niño otra vez?
> Niño para mi madre: me lo dice tu beso.
> Yo sigo oyendo el mismo cuento de mi niñez.
> Mi niñez fué sombría. Sólo tu cuento era
> distracción, madre mía, de tal niñez . . . ¿Quizás
> es niño alguien sin juego, ni risa, ni carrera?
> Por lo mismo que nunca lo fuí como debiera,
> ya sé que no he dejado de ser niño jamás.
> Así es como esta noche te diré, madre mía,
> que al regresar del viaje que en mi busca emprendí,

he venido a encontrarme contigo todavía,
como si no me hubiera separado de ti.

The "Nocturnos" which revolve around his home, with his mother as the central, beloved figure listening to his words, put aside pretense and ostentation, and are tinged with sadness.

"Nocturno de la coronación" closes the last volume of *Oro de Indias*. Written in Lima in 1924, the poem is filled with the deep pain that accompanies the remembrance of past glories when the inevitable decline is sensed. "I am alone . . . and the vision of other things comes to my eyes: the crown of thorns, the wreath of roses. I remember that many times I have seen the roses of Epicurus around my head. . . . Now I find only the crown of thorns that cause me to bleed internally. . . . But when I close my eyes to see into my soul, I should like to give my lyre a moment of rest and to be, away from everything, completely myself. For glory has, like pleasure, its weariness":

> Estoy sólo . . .
> Y así, a mis ojos viene la visión de otras cosas:
> la corona de espinas, la guirnalda de rosas.
> Recuerdo que hartas veces en mis sienes he visto
> las rosas de Epicuro . . .
> . . . ya solamente encuentro
> la corona de espinas que me sangran por dentro.
> . . . .
> pero al cerrar los ojos para mirarme el alma,
> bien quisiera a mi lira darle un rato de calma
> y ser, lejos de todos, completamente mío,
> porque la gloria tiene, como el placer, su hastío.

We cannot know whether Chocano himself would have chosen this "Nocturno" as his final offering, but it is an appropriate ending for four volumes of poetry that encompass more than twenty-six years of the poet's life, passing through periods of great glory and fervent admiration, and rancorous, bitter accusations and hatreds.

The final work of Chocano permits us to hear his lyricism, so long drowned out by the loud trumpeting of his epic songs. The arrogant Chocano of *Alma América* covered this vein of lyric tenderness and allowed only an occasional glimpse in *¡Fiat Lux!* But the sufferings of this proud spirit, whether set in motion by himself or not, awakened the dormant lyric qualities which had been stifled by the dramatic aspects of his art. Now the image of a despotic, contemptuous Chocano has been softened. Now we have the Chocano of sensitive poetry together with the Chocano of robust verse—the complete epic-lyric poet.

CHAPTER 6

Poet of America?

POET OF AMERICA was the title given to Chocano after the triumph of his *Alma América* in 1906. The delighted Spanish audiences and the flattered Latin Americans—particularly Peruvians—saw the content of *Alma América* as a glowing expression of authentic Spanish Americanism, and Chocano as the authentic spokesman.

The mantle of adulation fitted Chocano easily, and in fact had belonged to him in his own country from early youth. Few poets have reaped the spectacular acclaim which followed Chocano all the way into the 1920's. The colorful figure of both the man and the poet projected his image upon the public—an image which in many ways was representative of the last vestiges of a violent and seething nineteenth-century Spanish America.

The collapse of Chocano's fame was abrupt and complete. Few poets have received the invectives and abuse that were heaped on Chocano personally from the middle 1920's until his death, and which continued for some time at the same pace until subsiding into mere scorn.

His own country mirrors the reasons for this amazing shift of appreciation. Indeed, the Peruvian backdrop set the stage for this decline. While Chocano, the poet, still reigned supreme at his "Coronation" in 1922, there were young writers of that period who were earnestly searching for new literary avenues and who often turned for inspiration to purely Peruvian themes in their attempts to break away from the Chocanesque style in which Peruvian poetry had been submerged since the beginning of the twentieth century. Gradually a social awareness was creeping into the literature, bringing with it a new, realistic note which was concerned with the vast indigenous majority in Peru. The idea that Peruvian poetry should be rooted in the land and in the human problems of

Peru flowered into the appearance of Nativism and Indigenism around 1926. Chocano could not, or would not, merge with this new emphasis, and he made no concessions to the searching restlessness in his country. Instead he remained faithful to his own style of poetry in which he had no peer;[1] and in politics he made no secret of his alliance on the side of responsible dictatorships. Thus he came to defend a position in ideological opposition to the new generation. Smoldering resentment burst into the flames of hatred after the Elmore tragedy. Chocano, the Poet Laureate of Peru, became the fallen idol of his country.

The shift in Peruvian opinion gives a magnified look at the swing in world opinion. Normally the quality of a poet's life should not greatly affect the critiques of his work, particularly as these move out of the sphere of contemporary time and personal contact. Yet for many years Chocano's work seemed to be judged almost entirely in the light of his life. This current was followed by Arturo Torres-Ríoseco, who began an essay on Chocano by stating: "Now that the poet laureate of Peru has died, there is the obligation of dedicating the study to him which we have always denied because his life was the negation of the ideal that we hold for the mission of the poet. . . . His was a violent life, more than it should have been for a cultivator of beauty. . . . He adulated the tyrants of our continent and he paid dearly for this adulation."[2] After 1926 most of Chocano's critics discussed his poetry solely in this spirit, a fact which has had a lasting effect upon the poet's place in Spanish American literature. Few indeed were able to take the position of José Vasconcelos which he expressed in Buenos Aires immediately after the poet's death: "Before Chocano's tomb we must forget the Man and pay reverence to the fame of the Great Poet."[3]

In view of this animosity toward Chocano, it is sometimes difficult to separate hostile personal and political criticism from valid literary criticism. There were, however, intellectual as well as emotional reasons for the changed attitudes toward Chocano's poetry, and the literary aspects must be carefully considered in some sequence.

The title "Poet of America" clung tenaciously to Chocano after his triumph in Spain, and for many years on both sides of the Atlantic it continued to mean that Chocano was the principal representative of Americanism in the contemporary poetry of Spanish America. In the first flush of success after *Alma América* no one questioned the authenticity of the American scene as Chocano painted it, least of all those *limeños* basking in the reflected glory of their poet. The descriptions of nature in the American world—fundamental in Chocano's work—were so overwhelming in their abundance and magnificence that they seemed to everyone to be of indisputable authority. It is easy to appreciate the rapt Spanish critics who thought they were seeing both the true American landscape in all its lush beauty, and the true sentiment and spirit of the New World in the nostalgic longing for a glorious past of the viceroyalty or Inca empire. Unamuno thanked Chocano for taking him to America and showing him the exotic and overpowering panoramas of another world, and he identified Chocano as the poet from "the most Spanish of American countries . . . from that sweet and tepid Peru where the tradition of the viceroyalty still lingers, where after the Incaic magnificence came the viceroy elegance."[4] Such a confusion between Lima, the frivolous, proud capital, and Peru, a country of striking environmental and cultural contrasts, passed unnoticed in 1906.

North American critics looked upon Chocano as a new force in Spanish American poetry, and they found the title "Poet of America" entirely suitable. George Umphrey (1920),[5] for example, not only accepted the authenticity of Chocano's Americanism, but he attributed considerable depth to it because in his opinion Chocano aspired to give a poetic interpretation of Spanish American life in all its phases: past, present, future, Spanish, indigenous, historical, and descriptive. In that same year Isaac Goldberg wrote: "The book [*Alma América*] is in remarkable degree the soul of the continent for which it speaks: it is spiritual history. If the foreign reader seeks a single book that will communicate to him the complex Spanish American soul, here it is."[6] As late as 1928 Alfred Coester continued in this vein: "In the present generation of writers Peru has given the world one of the dominating figures of the latest phase of Spanish-American literature, José Santos Chocano. Though his works have their roots in Peruvian soil their fruits have been shared by the whole Spanish-American world."[7]

In Latin America the glad songs of praise for the "Poet of America" began to change key, almost imperceptibly at first, but rising slowly to a loud chorus of dissonance. A considerable part of Chocano's fame rested on the glittering beauty and imagination of his torrents of descriptive verse, but it was this aspect which earliest began to pall. Peruvians, at first so proud of their poet, were especially harsh in their criticism. Intellectuals in Peru, increasingly cognizant of their country's reality, became disconcerted by what they considered to be showy metaphors and hollow imagery. They were uncomfortably aware that Chocano's spiritual and environmental formation belonged entirely to the mild coast of Lima, and thus it was with the soul of a *limeño* that he poured out his verses of Andean imagery so full of immense peaks and barren plateaus and plunging rivers which he had beheld in astonishment only once! The rich fantasy that saw the Andes as "heroes who rise with granite shields" and send downward the "silent tear of a river" held no magic for the Peruvian intellectual of the 1920's, so imbued with an insistence on reality. Ventura García Calderón, well-known Peruvian writer and Chocano's contemporary, began as early as 1910 to find fault with Chocano's extravagances of description.[8] Ten years later his criticism was much sharper and he disparaged the unfeeling, exterior quality of Chocano's descriptive talent.[9] (However, he sustained Chocano's supremacy as the Continent's most powerful poet and Peru's "most certain glory.")

Beginning in the late 1920's, and fanned by the ill-will so evident against the man, it became the fashion to ridicule everything Chocanesque, particularly his descriptions. To show their scorn, Spanish American critics used terms like cinematographic nature, hallucinated visions, literary fabrications, stereotyped, ingenious imitations of reality, and they even descended to witticisms which implied that Chocano wrote hanging from his feet! Typical of such devastating comments are: "Chocano sees the American world with powerful field glasses and expresses it as though he had contemplated the scene by using the reverse end of the glasses" (Torres-Ríoseco).[10] "The American world of Chocano is revealed in its true cardboard texture. Chocano's masterpiece is in his indexes; he should never have gone beyond the titles" (Fernando Alegría).[11]

To Peruvians the question of the *depth* of Chocano's vision was of much more importance than a discussion of his descriptive art. In Peru the presence of nature had always entered into the literature, and therefore since earliest colonial times Peruvian writers had developed an intense descriptive power. In his own way Chocano was the culmination of this quality. The new Peruvian writers emerging in the 1920's, however, began to delve into the meaning and impact of the environment. This placed Chocano in opposition to them, for he made no attempt to penetrate beyond the outer wrappings. When Chocano confronts the Andes, the telluric immensity overwhelms him to the extent of making him ignore that there is a forgotten nation living within this "sculptured serpent." For Chocano, the Andes do not speak. The awesome silence and loneliness inspires his metaphoric verse, but he is an eloquent spectator without any understanding, without even the desire to understand. His imaginative descriptions of the Andes contrast sharply with the Andean landscapes of the following generations which portray the imposing strength of nature together with the desperation and tragedy of the man existing there.

The new Peruvian writers, directing their creative force in search of true identification with the land and the people, came to center all their attention upon the indigenous problem of the country. These "Nativists"[12] went so far as to insist that the autochthonous constituted the nucleus of Peru. From the time of the Conquest until Chocano's era, all history and culture of Peru had belonged to the coastal area and to the Spanish environment of that region. As part of the social revolution, the new generation had only scorn for those past colonial aspects, particularly the *limeña* attitude which Chocano typified.

It is in the treatment of the Indian theme, therefore, where the deepest chasm exists between Chocano and later Peruvian writers. Chocano, like the conquerors, uses the Indian to provide richness and color for his poetic empire. Only the sumptuousness and grandeur of a fantastic kingdom, or the heroic attributes of famous Indian warriors, really hold any interest for this Peruvian poet. Of all the writers who have used the Indian for decorative purposes, no one treats the subject with more personal good fortune than Chocano. From his *El Derrumbe* (1899) through the last volumes of his poetry, the Indian element acquires richness and artistic refinement, but there is no capturing of the Indian spirit. The Indian is sober and impassive. Chocano is his antithesis. We see clearly the radiant figure of the conqueror, but not the tragic darkness of the conquered.

For Chocano the Indian is a picturesque legend, and his lost empire, a dazzling vision. The poet prefers to ignore the degradation of the descendants. Out of the immensity of Chocano's *indigenista* work, only four poems, "Notes of the Indigenous Soul" (discussed in Chapter 5), convey a fleeting impression that he was aware of the pitiful state of the Indian in his country. "Yet even here, where he has the Indian reality within his reach, he cannot grasp it, much less interpret it."[13] Throughout these four poems it never occurs to the poet that the Indian's frugality of speech, his apparent resignation in the answers "Who knows, Señor," or "So be it," stems from a full understanding of the questioner. Four centuries of oppression have taught the Indian to expect nothing and to ask for nothing. It is impossible for Chocano to identify with this Indian. Instead, the poet seems bewildered by his plight, so far removed from the way he wishes to view him. The most he can do even in his "Notes of the Indigenous Soul" is to compromise by equating the enigmatic sadness of the Indian with his own state of sadness.

Foreign writers have sometimes mistakenly credited Chocano with having a part in the social changes sweeping over the Indian countries of Latin America. One American critic in 1946 even went so far as to write: "His voice was the cry of the mestizo shouting out defiance to the paler white man."[14] Coupled with an innocent acceptance of the poet's mestizo blood, most North American critics believe that the "Notes of the Indigenous Soul" represent a radical departure from the arrogant and egotistic conqueror of old. Hence they are apt to terminate their critiques with statements such as: "It is a changed Chocano who is speaking . . . his studies of native manners are marked by a sympathetic insight as pleasing as it is unexpected."[15]

By contrast, Peruvians find no understanding of the Indian anywhere in Chocano's poetry. For them Chocano always remains the conqueror talking to the conquered, the lord who stops to question his peon, who wonders for an instant about another creature—not an equal—before returning to his own environment. Part of this inability to accept Chocano's sincerity lies in their proximity to the situation and their first hand information. Chocano often proclaimed himself the son of the Inca—"My blood indeed is Spanish, but Incaic its pulsation"—which the rest of the world took to signify that he was a true mestizo. To Peruvians this was pure nonesense. García Calderón neatly punctured this concept in 1920: "To show his almost ancestral love of the New World he [Chocano] goes around swearing he is half Indian when we all know his origin is only Spanish."[16] In his *Memorias*, written in 1930–31,

Chocano himself says carefully that he *supposes* he has Indian blood on both sides of his family.[17] Perhaps he said this as a rebuke to his Peruvian critics, or perhaps he wished to enlist himself in the popular trend of his day. It was really not of great importance. Chocano was of Spanish intellectual and spiritual formation, and his countrymen were acutely aware of this. When he attempted some poetic identification with the Indian, it only infuriated them. Nothing is more incorrect than to think that Chocano was a mestizo and for that reason able to interpret the Indian spirit. The more foreign praise Chocano received for his sympathetic interpretation of the Indian, the more clenched fists were raised against him in Peru.

The abuse that Chocano received in his last years does not negate the great popularity which was his during the major part of his lifetime. Until the mid-1920's he was one of the most forceful literary voices of Latin America. The "singer of autochthonous and savage America" exulted the glories of the Continent, praised her heroes, painted her beauty; and the ringing music of his exuberant poetry brought forth a deep continental response. Chocano was the culmination of the flavor of his society. When new forces swept aside his literary figures and his political and social ideas, when he no longer represented the dominant pattern of life, he fell from his pedestal. His own country was the first to lift him up and the first to tear him down. Luis Alberto Sánchez, a Peruvian of the generation which followed Chocano, exemplifies the sweep of the pendulum. With unrestrained fervor the young Sánchez hailed Chocano at his 1922 "Coronation": "Our father who art in verse. . . . Eponym poet of a boiling Continent, maximum poet of a superlative race, incommensurable poet in a country of gnomes . . . a poet above thousands of poets . . . Chocano is love of the land, pride of a race, fruition of the past, boundless ardor for our Continent. . . . Pray with me Spanish Americans: Our father who art in verse, may your name be glorified now and forever. Amen."[18] Almost a quarter of a century later, in 1946,[19] this same writer referred to Chocano as a poet who merely expressed himself through exterior descriptions, in contrast to later poets of deep penetration who offer the authentic interpretation of the landscape and the man of the sierra.

Most Peruvians continued to judge Chocano's work from an intensely personal viewpoint through the 1940's. Eventually this gave way to less emotional outbursts, although he continued to be either scoffed at or curtly dismissed. In 1954 Sánchez published *José Santos Chocano. Obras completas* (in Mexico), with his own extensive and surprisingly mellow explanations of Chocano's life and work. Of interest is his comment that he received help everywhere except in Peru! In 1962 an anthology entitled *José Santos Chocano. Sus mejores poemas* appeared in Lima, edited by Francisco Bendezú, poet and professor of literature in San Marcos University. The volume is small, and the reader may not agree with the selections, but the prologue is the first balanced view of Chocano's work by a Peruvian and sets forth both strong points and defects in Chocano's poetry. Without apology Bendezú states his opinion: "I consider Chocano a valuable poet, of great importance in Peru and America, but not an extraordinary genius."[20] Perhaps the pendulum has ceased its wild swinging. The Peruvian generation following Chocano loathed him for political and personal reasons, but new Peruvian generations, unaffected by emotional entanglements, may come to appreciate what he represented for the Peru of his day.

In attempting to assess Chocano's true position in Spanish American literature, it is necessary to withdraw somewhat from the heat and controversy that his name engenders in his own country. Is he a great poet? Does he deserve to be known as "Poet of America"?

It cannot be denied that much of Chocano's work suffers not only from the superficiality so decried by Peruvians, but perhaps even more from his oratorical emphasis, the noise of cymbals and drums, the exorbitant heroism. In much of his poetry Chocano is like the geraniums of his own Lima, colorful, lush, springing up with tropical ease of growth even in shallow soil. The iridescent froth and foam of these poems is pleasing even though a prick of the finger will break the shining bubbles. By contrast, Chocano can rise to be a superior painter of the seductive and exotic beauty of American nature, and he is capable of reaching occasional heights of poetic magnificence. The ego in his poetry is unrestrained. He is often bombastic, trite, and irritating. Yet amid all the glittering sequins and the tinseled verbosity there are moments when he is unaffected, natural, and touchingly beautiful.

Many reproach Chocano for the lack of intimate feeling in his poetry. Certainly there is an objective, exterior quality in the major part of his poetic work. Yet in the midst of the excitement and the waving banners of his processions, there are sudden clearings of unsuspected simplicity and tender lyricism. The glimpses are brief, but they suggest possibilities in his art that never came to full bloom. The disillusions and reversals of fortune toward the end of his life enriched the soil for the flowering of his intimate "Nocturnos" and the other sensitive poetry of those years. Unfortunately by that time the parade had already passed by, and relatively few turned around for more than a glance. Chocano has never received full attention or a just evaluation of his last poetry. As a triumphant poet he had inspired awe but never affection, and there was no residue of warmth or compassion left to greet these final, moving poems.

Chocano's dramatic and premature success in his own country fostered his extraordinary self-complacency and pride, which in turn fanned his insatiable desire for fame. In part Chocano missed the heights of lasting greatness which might have been his because he squandered his energies in incessant action. Within Chocano existed the shadow of a great poet who never knew how to emerge from the superfluous.

To accept this loss of the highest laurels does not, however, justify the view that Chocano is an outmoded songster of little value, a cheap versifier of the plaza, a sculptor in sand. This is to ignore his considerable impact on Peruvian and continental poetry. The new direction which Chocano gave to Modernism and the telluric American note which he injected into this movement cannot be subtracted from his glory. With all his limitations these contributions balance the scale in favor of considering him a major and irreplaceable figure in Spanish American letters.

"Poet of America," the title bestowed on Chocano at the beginning of the twentieth century, recognized this poet as Spanish America's principal spokesman. It is a fitting title in the sense that Chocano does represent most fully the America of his time—that objective, visible, seething world of late nineteenth-century Spanish America which continued well into this century. Chocano's poetry is full of regional and continental sensations as he saw and felt them. There is no more reason to doubt his sincerity and to sneer because he did not penetrate in the manner we expect from today's writers than there is to criticize any writer of another day because he did not face our contemporary world.

Much of Chocano's work does not transcend his own era. Many of the fading watercolors of his two-dimensional poetry will be forgotten in the future. But from his best poems a brilliant anthology could be compiled which would keep the luster of his poetic name shining for new generations of Americans—a pride for Peru and for Spanish America.

Notes and References

Chapter One

1. *Obras completas. Memorias. Las mil y una aventuras* (Mexico, 1954), pp. 1400, 1402. In this chapter all quotations of Chocano's own words are from his *Memorias* (*Obras completas*), unless otherwise indicated, and have been translated into English by the present author. Chocano refers to: War of the Pacific, 1879–84; Spanish American War, 1898; Independence of Panama, 1903; intervention of the United States in Cuba, 1906–1909; end of Zelaya's rule, 1909; Mexican Revolution, 1910–20; assassination of Madero, 1913; of Carranza, 1920 (after Chocano had left Mexico); fall of Estrada Cabrera, 1920; centennial of the Battle of Ayacucho, 1924; treaty of Tacna and Arica, 1929. The imprisonments were in Callao, 1894–95; in Guatemala, 1920; in Lima, 1925–27.

2. *Ibid.*, p. 1403.

3. *Ibid.*, p. 1413.

4. Among his school companions were Clemente Palma, a son of Ricardo Palma; Luis Aurelio Loayza; and the father of Luis Alberto Sánchez.

5. The novel *Aves sin nido*, by Clorinda Matto de Turner, was a virulent protest against the situation of the Peruvian Indian as well as an attack on the clergy. Published in 1889, it touched off a storm of controversy in Peru.

6. It was in this fortress that the poet's father had been decorated for his valor in defending the country against bombardment by the Spanish (1866). One of Chocano's guards was his enemy Joaquín Miró Quesada (a close relative of a future enemy, an owner and publisher of *El Comercio*) who had expressly offered his services. Another jailer was Captain Benavides, who became President of Peru. Imprisoned with Chocano was José Domingo Parra, father of the poet Juan Parra del Riego.

7. The verses of *Iras santas* were written between 1893 and 1895, while those of *En la aldea* were completed for the most part in 1893. Nevertheless bibliographies place *Iras* in the first position because the poet set them in this order in his *Poesías completas* (1902).

8. At the Second Panamerican Congress, Mexico, October, 1901–January, 1902, a treaty on compulsory arbitration was drawn up, but signed by only nine delegations.

9. General Regalado's successor, already elected, was Pedro Escalón, and it was he who met with Estrada Cabrera on board ship. Although peace was assured at this time, war broke out three years later.

10. *Antología poética* (Buenos Aires, 1948), p. 16.

11. *Obras completas*, p. 24.

12. "Fin de raza" (1908), *Oro de Indias* (Santiago de Chile), 1940.

13. "Oda salvaje" (probably 1908), *Poemas escogidos* (Paris, 1912) and *Oro de Indias*.

14. *Antología poética*, p. 17.

15. Attributed to José Vasconcelos in *Páginas de oro* (Lima, 1944), p. 62.

16. Originally told by Luis Berninzone in *Chocano al rojo* (Santiago, 1938) and quoted by Escudero, pp. 17–18, Sánchez, p. 27, and Xammar, p. lil, in their respective prologues. Berninzone, a Peruvian, accompanied Chocano when he left Peru in 1928 to live in Chile.

17. "Prólogo interior," version of *El Dorado* (Cuba, 1908).

18. Chocano made this statement: "The people are right to ask for my head, since they have never had one." *Páginas de oro*, p. 75.

19. *Obras completas*, p. 30, and *Antología poética*, p. 18.

20. *La coronación de José Santos Chocano* (Lima, 1924) gives details of the ceremonies. In later years Peruvian writers hastened over the "Coronation" as though embarrassed by the display of excess emotion.

21. Alfred Coester, *An Anthology of the Modernista Movement in Spanish America* (Boston, 1924), p. 305.

22. *Obras completas*, p. 32.

23. The most extensive material concerning the Elmore incident comes from Peruvian writers. Since they are emotionally involved, the information is highly colored in one direction or the other.

24. *Antología poética*, pp. 19–20.

25. Account given by Sánchez, Peruvian, in *Obras completas*, pp. 32–33. According to Sánchez, Chocano is supposed to have turned to one of his admirers and said: "I have immortalized a nobody."

26. Account given by Escudero, Chilean, in *Antología poética*, p. 20. Chocano's wife, Margarita, has a different version in her book, *José Santos Chocano, sus últimos años*, (Lima, 1965), pp. 133–37. She states that she was waiting outside while the poet stopped at the *Comercio* offices to deliver an article. Hearing a shot, she rushed in to find Chocano bleeding from a facial wound and Elmore staggering toward the door. The poet assured her that although he had had to defend himself, he had fired at the floor.

27. "Serenamente" (1926?), *El libro de mi proceso* (Lima, 1927–28), and *Primicias de oro de Indias* (Santiago de Chile, 1934).

28. "La gloria del proceso," originally published in *Poemas escogidos* (1912) and then in *El libro de mi proceso* (1927–28).

29. *Obras completas* (*El libro de mi proceso*), p. 1130.
30. *Obras completas*, pp. 1086–87.
31. Margarita expressly denies this, stating that the poet kept the crown with the intention of giving it to their son. She was unable to carry out his wishes.
32. "Finigénito" (1934), *Primicias de oro de Indias*.
33. As described to me by an eyewitness.
34. Margarita's version differs in that she says Chocano was able to walk down the steps of the streetcar, thus precipitating the hemorrhaging.
35. Margarita writes that Badilla had been obsessed for sometime with the idea that Chocano could obtain permission for him to dig for buried treasure which had been shown to him in a vision. She believes Badilla confused the festivities over Chocano's *Primicias* with the idea that Chocano had obtained everything by finding the treasure himself.
36. "Lucha y trabajo," *Iras santas* (Lima, 1895).
37. Details from *El Comercio*, Lima, May 16, 1965.
38. Expressed in his poem "La vida náufraga." See Chap. 5, p. 127.
39. *Memorias*, p. 1400.
40. "Ultima rebelión" (1920?), *Oro de Indias*.
41. "Espaldarazo," *Primicias de oro de Indias*.
42. *Obras completas*, p. 12

Chapter Two

1. "Desde la cumbre," *Iras santas* (Lima, 1895).
2. "Catilinaria," *Iras santas*.
3. "Desde la cumbre," *Iras santas*.
4. "A Lázaro," *Iras santas*.
5. "Para todos," *Iras santas*.
6. Phyllis Rodríguez-Peralta, "The Perú of Chocano and Vallejo," *Hispania*, Vol. XLIV, no. 4 (Dec. 1961), p. 639.
7. Examples come from the following poems of *En la aldea* (Lima, 1895): "El Sapo," "Paisaje," "La Carretera," "En el templo."
8. "Resurrección," *En la aldea*.
9. Prologue to *Poesías completas* (Barcelona, 1902).
10. "Sinfonía de amor," *Azahares* (Lima, 1896). The lines are strongly reminiscent of "A Gloria" (1884), by Salvador Díaz Mirón.
11. "El séptimo día," *Azahares*.
12. The first edition of *Selva virgen* was probably published in Lima, 1896, a date mentioned in a few bibliographies but without publication details. Three subsequent Paris editions are each noticeably augmented with new poems dated 1898, 1899, 1900.
13. "Canto III," *La epopeya del Morro* (Lima, 1899).
14. "Canto VII," *La epopeya del Morro*.

15. Examples from *La epopeya del Morro:* "Canto I," "*Ibid.*," "Canto III," "Canto VI," "Canto VII."

16. "Canto II," *La epopeya del Morro.*

17. Luis Alberto Sánchez makes a great point of these suppressions, illustrating the intimate attitude with which this well-known Peruvian writer (and many other Peruvians) views Chocano's work. Sánchez maintains that the hostility of a certain critic, mentioned by name, stems precisely from the fact that in the final version of *La epopeya del Morro* Chocano omitted the illustrious deeds by his relative of the same name.

18. Suppressed from *En la aldea* are: "La Invasión" (a notoriously anti-Chilean sonnet), "Mañana alegre," "Aquí," "La Estatua," "Todo muere," "En el templo," "La Cabra," "La Vid," "Matinal," "Música," "La Oración," "Indiana."

19. The final "El amor de las selvas," which appears again in *Alma América* with various suppressions.

20. González Prada believed that he saw a true crusader in the young poet of *Iras santas* who railed against tyranny and advocated the brotherhood of man. But the years have revealed that the poet's hatred was for a particular tyrant. The poet's democratic idealism faded when he became convinced that this would lead to mediocrity.

21. The first "Postdata" was a section of five poems attached to *El fin de Satán y otros poemas:* "Estigma," "A Panamá," "Alma fuerte," "Sol y luna," "El Rayo." The "Postdata" of *Los cantos del Pacífico* contains four of these, excluding "A Panamá," plus three additional: "Yunque," "Incontrastable," and "Proclama." The eighth is "Fragmentos de un poema" which appeared in another section of *El fin de Satán.*

22. "Indudablemente Rubén Darío no es el poeta de América" (Certainly Rubén Darío is not the poet of America) is Rodó's well-known phrase from his essay on *Prosas profanas* (1896), written in 1899 (*Hombres de América,* 1920).

Chapter Three

1. "Tríptico heroico. II. Cuacthemoc," *Alma América* (Madrid–Paris, 1906).

2. *Ibid.,* I.

3. "Cahuide."

4. Phyllis Rodríguez-Peralta, *op. cit.,* p. 636.

5. "La tierra del sol. III. Coloniaje," *op. cit.*

6. In his *Memorias* Chocano says that he had been chatting with Benito Pérez Galdós about things typical of Lima and that he offered to summarize everything in a poem. This became "Ciudad colonial," which he dedicated to Pérez Galdós.

7. Phyllis Rodríguez-Peralta, *op. cit.,* p. 636.

8. "La tierra del sol. III. Coloniaje," *op. cit.*

9. *La tapada*, a term from the times of the viceroyalty, describes a woman of Lima, dressed in a long, full skirt, with a shawl draped artistically over her head so that only one coquettish eye could be seen.

10. "Ante las ruinas," *op. cit.*

11. "El Istmo de Panamá," *op. cit.*

12. "El canto del porvenir," *op. cit.*

13. In *Studies in Spanish-American Literature* (New York, 1920), Isaac Goldberg writes: "Together with the Darío of the *Canto á la Argentina* he [Chocano] represents the most favorable attitude toward us among the prominent poets." p. 290.

14. "La Quena," *op. cit.*

15. These lines in *Alma América* contain only two minor changes from the original form used in *El canto del siglo*.

16. "Símbolo," *op. cit.*

17. "Avatar," *op. cit.*

18. *Ibid.*

19. "Troquel," *op. cit.*

20. "La musa fuerte," *op. cit.*

21. From the prologue by Unamuno, Madrid edition.

22. "La epopeya del Pacífico," *op. cit.*

23. "El mediodía en el istmo," *op. cit.*

24. "Tríptico heroico. II. Cuacthemoc," *op. cit.*

25. "El idilio de los cóndores," *op. cit.*

26. "Los Ríos," *op. cit.*

27. "Los Pantanos," *op. cit.*

28. "La elegía del órgano," *op. cit.*

29. "Bajando la cuesta," *op. cit.*

30. "Los Lagos," *op. cit.*

31. "Evangeleida," *op. cit.*

32. "Crónica alfonsina," *op. cit.*

33. Darío included this "Preludio" in his *El canto errante* (1907), but with two additional lines at the end: "Tal dije cuando don J. Santos Chocano,/último de los Incas, se tornó castellano." These were either added later by Darío or pared from the original by Chocano. If the latter version is the correct one, it shows Chocano's good taste, for the lines detract from the poem. In any case, Chocano would have intensely disliked the reference to his "becoming Castilian."

34. Chocano lists a brief selection of early poems: *El Dorado: Epopeya salvaje;* and *Romancero de Indias: Leyendas americanas.*

35. Phyllis Rodríguez-Peralta, *op. cit.*, p. 640.

36. Juan Ramón Jiménez called this the era of *chocaneros*, a scornful expression more for the imitators than for Chocano.

37. Prologue to the Madrid edition.

38. "La vejez anacreóntica," "Estandarte de amor," "Sátira," "Onomástico," "Urna," "Pagana," "Copa de oro," "El retrato de César," "Arqueología," "El último canto de Nerón."

39. From "Postdata:" "El Rayo" and "Sol y luna"; from *Selva virgen:* "De viaje," "Declamatorio," "El nuevo dodecasílabo," "El Cofre"; from *En la aldea:* "En la alcoba," "Paisaje."

40. The last three poems of Part IV: "En elogio de Daoiz," "La lucha inútil," "El arco de Ulises"; and the five "Sonetos necrológicos" dedicated to Espronceda.

Chapter Four

1. Darío himself states in his *Historia de mis libros* that he read the French works in translation and with the help of Baralt's *Diccionario de galicismos.*

2. The new writers had used the word *moderno* to be distinguished from *tradición.* Disparagingly their opponents coined the word *modernista,* and from this came the term *modernismo* for the entire movement.

3. Nájera, 1859–95; Díaz Mirón, 1853–1928; Martí, 1853–95; Casal, 1863–93; Silva 1865–96.

4. Literary journals which achieved a solid reputation: *La Revista de América,* Buenos Aires, 1896, founded by Darío and Jaimes Freyre; *La Revista Azul,* Mexico, 1894–96, founded by Gutiérrez Nájera and Díaz Dufóo; *La Revista Moderna,* Mexico, 1898–1903, 1903–11, founded by Amado Nervo and Valenzuela. See Chap. 1, pp. 22–23, for others which flourished during this epoch.

5. Darío, Nicaragua, 1867–1916; Nervo, 1870–1919; Lugones, 1874–1938; Jaimes Freyre, 1868–1933; Herrera y Reissig, 1875–1910; Chocano, 1875–1934. A more extensive list usually includes José María Eguren of Peru, 1874? 1882?–1942, Guillermo Valencia of Colombia, 1873–1943, and Enrique González Martínez of Mexico, 1871–1952. Although this group includes only poets, at least two prose writers must be mentioned: José Enrique Rodó, Uruguay, 1872–1917, and Manuel Díaz Rodríguez, Venezuela, 1868–1927.

6. A Chilean, Francisco Contreras, invented the name *mundonovismo* to signify this adaptation of Modernism to the autochthonous.

7. Ricardo Palma, 1833–1919; Manuel González Prada, 1848–1918.

8. *Historia de la literatura hispanoamericana* (Mexico, 1957), pp. 282–83.

9. *Ensayos sobre literatura latinoamericana* (Berkeley, 1953), p. 180.

10. *36 Spanish Poems* (Boston, 1957), p. 60.

11. *Studies in Spanish-American Literature* (New York, 1920), p. 297.

12. *Obras completas (Memorias),* pp. 1453–54.

13. *Antología poética,* p. 13.

14. Quoted from G. Dundas Craig, *The Modernist Trend in Spanish-American Poetry* (Berkeley, 1934), p. 19.

15. "Leticiae."

16. See Chap. 3, p. 71, for English summary of Chocano's poem.

17. George Umphrey compared the poetry of these two "exultant, exuberant poets from the New World" in an article entitled "José Santos Chocano, 'el Poeta de América'," (*Hispania*, Vol. III, no. 6 [Dec., 1920]), which was translated into Spanish and extensively circulated in South America. Written in 1920, Umphrey based most of his comments on Chocano's work up to 1908. While he admits that Chocano is not democratic nor fraternal nor a literary anarchist (and therefore the title of "the Walt Whitman of South America" should be used with reservations), he does accept Chocano's Americanism and even attributes wider breadth to this than to the Americanism of Whitman. In his *Memorias* (1930–31) Chocano states that Umphrey indeed penetrated into his "individualistic and hierarchic spirit."

Fernando Alegría (*Walt Whitman en Hispanoamérica* [Mexico, 1954]) feels that the only reason anyone has to insist upon the obvious differences between Chocano and Whitman is precisely because Umphrey's article was so well known that his ideas were perpetuated. Alegría even goes so far as to hint that Chocano really knew little about Whitman until it became the style to liken him to the American poet. This latter idea, however, seems unlikely considering the general admiration of the Modernists for Whitman and their continuous effect upon each other.

18. Baudelaire's French translation of Poe was widely circulated in Spanish America.

19. The early Díaz Mirón is completely different from his later, polished *Lascas*.

20. Martí's verse is often more tender and simple than one would suspect, while much of his prose is incendiary, like the man of action.

21. He lists: Darío, Lugones, Jaimes Freyre, Herrera y Reissig, Santos Chocano, Valencia, Nervo. *Op. cit.*, p. 291.

22. In 1911 Enrique González Martínez's sonnet "Tuércele el cuello al cisne" demanded that the swan's neck be wrung and that the intelligent owl replace the lovely but useless swan. Darío died in 1916. Ivory towers become tiresome and princesses are archaic. Today the dreamworld aspects of the Modernists seem as dated as the dashing Don Juans and fainting heroines of Romanticism. The enriching effects of Modernist techniques, however, are clearly visible in the distinguished Latin American poetry of this century.

Chapter Five

1. For example: George Umphrey, writing in 1920, mentions *El Dorado* (1908) but says that since that date there has been little fulfillment

of the promises, just scattered poems in periodicals; Isaac Goldberg, also
1920, discusses nothing after 1908, except for one poem in *Nosotros*, 1918;
Alfred Coester, 1924, includes "Tres notas de nuestra alma indigena,"
which he dates as 1922, but he adds that Chocano wrote very little after
Alma América.

2. "Epístola a Don Juan" (*Variedades* [Lima, 1909]). Will reappear
in *Primicias* (1934).

3. "Evócación," 1915, and "Prehistoria," 1918—Honduras, appear
again in *Primicias*. Chocano will recite "Plegaria lírica" at the "Coronation" celebrations, 1922. "Oda continental" had appeared in a Mexican
journal, 1917. These last two poems are inserted in *Oro de Indias*
(1939–41).

4. Apparently there was some dispute over payment, resulting in
the delay from November, 1922, until publication in 1924. This explains
the poems dated after the "Coronation" had taken place.

5. Chocano alters his 1,200,000 souls which greeted his representative
art in Puerto Rico to 5,000,000 in his "Coronation" speech! The portions
about art coming from history and nature and the section advocating
fidelity to one's own race and land are practically identical. See Chapter 1,
p. 35.

6. "Nocturnos: del regreso al hogar; de la copla callejera; del relato del
viaje; del reencuentro; del 'Hijo del rey'."

7. The work is some 1,565 lines in length. The poet varies the number
of syllables from four to twenty-one, in no pattern whatsoever, with
alternate assonantal rhyme of *e-a* throughout the entire poem.

8. The burning of the Biblioteca Nacional de Lima, May 10, 1943,
destroyed much of the literary work of the young Chocano. Among the
material lost was a complete collection from *La Neblina*, including many
irreplaceable selections of Chocano's early prose.

9. Among the prose pieces of *Idearium tropical* is "Sumario del
programa de la revolución mexicana." Chocano's activities during the
Mexican Revolution appeared to be in favor of the socially and economically oppressed. Actually, what fascinated him was the strength and
power of those who directed the movement. Chocano by nature was
always aligned with the leader.

10. The last extensive prose work during Chocano's lifetime was a
group of articles entitled *El escándalo de Leticia*, ninety-two pages dealing
with the frontier dispute between Peru and Colombia. *El alma de Voltaire
y otras prosas*, published by his wife in 1940, posthumously, is a collection
of some twenty-four diverse articles without explanatory notes or dates of
previous publications.

11. The Chilean years were from November, 1928, to his death in
December, 1934. The bibliography of *Obras completas* mentions a pamphlet
of poems entitled *Poemas chilenos del poeta peruano José Santos Chocano*

(Santiago, 1931?) as the poet's first attempt in Chile to recapture his fame. Unfortunately, no source could trace such a publication, including the *Anuario de la prensa chilena*.

12. A separate flier, *Muestrario lírico del Tomo II*, was inserted in each copy of *Primicias*. It was a kind of advertisement, consisting of one poem from each of the five remaining parts.

13. Appeared in *Poemas escogidos* (1912), not to be confused with the first poem of the same title in *Iras santas* (1895).

14. "Orgullo," originally from *Poemas escogidos* (1912).

15. The original version appeared in *El Dorado* (1908) and in the two subsequent collections of 1912 and 1914.

16. Published in a Yucatán journal, 1913.

17. From *El Dorado* (1908) (and 1912 and 1914). This also applies to the following "Dedicatoria."

18. *El libro de mi proceso* (1927–28). (Margarita states in her book that it had appeared in a San José daily in 1921.)

19. *El libro de mi proceso*.

20. Appeared in *Poemas escogidos* (1912).

21. Recited at "Coronation," 1922. His final burial position was decided according to this poem.

22. Their attraction began in 1921 when Chocano reached Costa Rica after being freed from prison and impending death. See Chap. 1, pp. 34 and 37.

23. As an example, two pages belonging to "Nocturno del hijo del rey" appear again in the midst of "Nocturno del viaje," and the latter itself reappears later in the collection!

24. The usual omission of original dates complicates the scene. The continuing antagonism among the three separate families which Chocano left has also blocked research.

25. Written in 1908, appeared in *Poemas escogidos* (1912).

26. Probably written in 1912. Appeared in a Mexican journal, 1917, and in *Poesías selectas* (1920?).

27. 1910. Appears in *Poemas escogidos* (1912).

28. 1914. An editorial note says this poem was read in the original Spanish, and in an English translation, at a ceremony honoring the poet which was given by the Poetry Society of America and the National Arts Club, New York, December 27, 1914.

29. *Poemas escogidos* (1912).

30. One poem from *Alma América*, a few from *¡Fiat Lux!*, and a few from *Primicias* are also added, with no apparent reason.

31. A note inserted by the poet says that he was severely criticized for describing the Mother Country in such a manner, but he defends his right to his own concepts, especially since he is "of the Spanish race."

32. Recited at his "Coronation," 1922, and included in *La coronación* (1924).

33. *Ibid.*

34. *Ibid.*, and also *Primicias* (1934) with title "El relato del viaje."

35. This "Nocturno" and the following "Nocturno de la coronación" appeared in the "Post-coronación" of *La coronación* (1924).

Chapter Six

1. Typical of Chocano's reaction to the new breed of writers was his disdain for César Vallejo, now considered one of Peru's finest poets. Chocano referred to him as "the poet without poems."

2. *Ensayos sobre literatura latinoamericana*, p. 172.

3. *Páginas de oro de José Santos Chocano*, p. 32

4. From Unamuno's prologue to *Alma América* (1906), Madrid edition.

5. "José Santos Chocano, 'el Poeta de América'," p. 315.

6. *Studies in Spanish-American Literature*, p. 292.

7. *An Anthology of the Modernista Movement in Spanish America*, p. 260.

8. *Del romanticismo al modernismo* (Paris, 1910), pp. 206–18.

9. *Semblanzas de América* (Madrid, 1920?), pp. 109–23.

10. *Ensayos sobre literatura latinoamerica*, p. 176.

11. *Walt Whitman en Hispanoamérica*, p. 276.

12. José Carlos Mariátegui, Luis E. Valcárcel, Uriel García, and others. Chocano held an opposite view from these writers. In his opinion, to say that only the Quechua race represents the true national spirit in Peru is as grotesque as to maintain that in the United States the only national spirit is that of the "redskins." (*El libro de mi proceso*, pp. 525–26.)

13. Phyllis Rodríguez-Peralta, *op. cit.*, p. 638.

14. John Crow, p. 540 of *An Anthology of Spanish American Literature*. (New York, 1946).

15. G. Dundas Craig, *op. cit.*, p. 309.

16 *Semblanzas*, p. 120.

17. *Obras completas. (Memorias)*, p. 1403.

18. *La coronación de José Santos Chocano*, pp. 38–44.

19. *La literatura peruana* (Lima, 1946), pp. 54–55.

20. *Sus mejores poemas* (Lima, 1962), p. 11.

Selected Bibliography

PRIMARY SOURCES

Principal Works of José Santos Chocano

Iras santas: poesías americanas. Lima: Imp. del Estado, 1895.
En la aldea: poesías americanas. Lima: Imp. del Estado, 1895.
Azahares. Lima: Imp. del Estado, 1896.
Selva virgen: poemas y poesías. Lima: Imp. del Estado, 1898?
La epopeya del Morro: poema americano. Lima: Ed. Iquique, Imp. Comercial, 1899.
El Derrumbe: poema americano. Lima, 1899.
El canto del siglo: poema finisecular. Prólogo de Emilio Gutiérrez de Quintanilla. Lima: Imp. La Industria, 1901.
El fin de Satán y otros poemas. Guatemala: Imp. en la Tipografía Nacional, 1901.
Poesías completas. Prólogo de Manuel González Prada. Barcelona: Edit. Maucci, 1902.
Los cantos del Pacífico: poesías selectas. Paris-Mexico: Librería Bouret, 1904.
Alma América: poemas indo-españoles. Prólogo de Miguel de Unamuno y Carta de M. Menéndez y Pelayo. Madrid: Ed. Suárez, 1906; y Paris: Librería Bouret, 1906.
¡Fiat Lux!: poemas varios. Prólogo de Andrés González Blanco. Madrid: Ed. Pueyo, 1908; y Paris: Librería Ollendorff, 1908.
El Dorado: epopeya salvaje. Fragmentos de un libro en preparación. Santiago de Cuba: E. Beltrán, 1908.
Poemas escogidos. Paris-Mexico: Librería Bouret, 1912.
Puerto Rico lírico y otros poemas. Prólogo de Luis Llorens Torres. San Juan de Puerto Rico: Edit. Antillana, 1914?
Poesías selectas. Prólogo de Ventura García Calderón. Paris: Franco-Ibero-Americano, 1920?
Idearium tropical. ("Apuntes sobre las dictaduras organizadoras y la gran farsa democrática"; "Ante los E.E.U.U. de América"; "El sumario del programa de la revolución mexicana.") Lima: Imp. La Opinión Nacional, 1922.

La coronación de José Santos Chocano. Lima: Imp. La Opinión Nacional, 1924.

Ayacucho y los Andes. Canto IV de *El Hombre Sol.* Lima: Pedro Berrio, 1924.

El libro de mi proceso. Tomo I, 1927; II y III, 1928. Lima: Imp. Americana de la Plazuela del Teatro; y Madrid: C(ompañía) I(bero) A(mericana) (de) P(ublicaciones), 1931.

Primicias de oro de Indias: poemas neo-mundiales. Santiago de Chile: Nascimento, 1937.

Poemas del amor doliente. Santiago de Chile: Nascimento, 1937.

Oro de Indias. Tomo I, 1939; II, 1940; III y IV, 1941. Santiago de Chile: Nascimento.

Memorias. Las mil y una aventuras. Santiago de Chile: Nascimento, 1940.

Anthologies and Collections

CHOCANO, JOSÉ SANTOS. *Antología poética.* Prólogo de Alfonso Escudero. Buenos Aires: Espasa-Calpe Argentina, 1948. Detailed and reliable. Very favorable to Chocano.

――――. *Obras completas.* Prólogo de Luis Alberto Sánchez. Mexico: Aguilar, 1954. Most complete work available. Gives many local details and intimate glimpses into Peruvian life.

――――. *Páginas de oro de José Santos Chocano.* Edición por Eduardo A. Chocano, hijo. Lima: Rimac, 1944. Curious mixture of adolescent verses, childhood memorabilia, and letters from the poet to his mother.

――――. *Poesías.* Colección Panamericana. Prólogo de Luis Fabio Xammar. Buenos Aires: Ediciones Jackson, 1945. Perceptive analysis and arrangement of Chocano's work.

――――. *Selección de Poesías.* Tomo I. Montevideo: Colección Cultura Claudio García, 1941. Contains collection of critiques by Juan Parra del Riego, M. González Prada, Isaac Goldberg, José Mariátegui, V. García Calderón, A. González Blanco, R. Meza Fuentes. Poorly edited with insufficient source data. Fantastic misinformation in critique of Parra de Riego.

――――. *Sus mejores poemas.* Prólogo de Francisco Bendezú. Lima: Editora Paracas, 1962. Excellent analysis of Chocano's work and his position in Spanish American literature.

Translations

BLACKWELL, ALICE STONE. *Some Spanish-American Poets.* Philadelphia: Univ. of Pennsylvania Press, 1937. Pp. 206–29.

CRAIG, G. DUNDAS. *The Modernist Trend in Spanish-American Poetry.* Berkeley: Univ. of California Press, 1934. Pp. 130–45, translations;

pp. 306–9, comments on Chocano's poetry; pp. 1–29, excellent introduction.

JONES, WILLIS KNAPP (Ed.). *Spanish-American Literature in Translation: A Selection of poetry, fiction, and drama since 1888.* New York: Frederick Ungar, 1963. Pp. 108–12.

Translations from Hispanic Poets. Hispanic Notes and Monographs. (Hispanic Society of America). New York, 1938. Pp. 252–55.

UNDERWOOD, EDNA WORTHLEY. *Spirit of the Andes: José Santos Chocano.* Portland, Maine: The Mosher Press, 1935.

University of Missouri Studies, XXIX, *Swan, Cygnets, and Owl: An Anthology of Modernist Poetry in Spanish America.* Columbia, Mo.: Univ. of Missouri Press, 1956. Mildred E. Johnson, translator. Pp. 108–11; introductory essay by J. S. Brushwood, pp. 1–33, is an excellent discussion of Modernism.

SECONDARY SOURCES

AGUILAR MACHADO, MARGARITA. *José Santos Chocano, sus últimos años.* Lima: Edit. Thesis, 1965. Poignant account of poet's last years, by his third wife.

ALEGRÍA, FERNANDO. *Walt Whitman en Hispanoamérica.* Mexico: Colección Studium, 1954. Pp. 276–81, discussion of Chocano and Whitman. Extremely critical of Chocano.

ANDERSON IMBERT, ENRIQUE. *Historia de la literatura hispanoamericana.* Mexico: Fondo de Cultura Económica, 1957. Pp. 282–83 and 328–29, brief discussion of Chocano's work, and Peruvian Modernist writers.

COESTER, ALFRED. *An Anthology of the Modernista Movement in Spanish America.* Boston: Ginn, 1924. Pp. 179–207, 304–7.

————. *The Literary History of Spanish America.* New York: Macmillan, 1928. Chap. VII, pp. 244–61; Chaps. XIV and XV, pp. 450–86. Good discussion of Peruvian writers after Independence to Chocano's era. Penetrating analysis of Modernist movement.

CRAIG, G. DUNDAS. See Translations.

ENGLEKIRK, JOHN E. *Edgar Allan Poe in Hispanic Literature.* New York: Instituto de las Españas, 1934. Pp. 394–96, brief discussion of few poems which show Poe's influence.

ENGLEKIRK, JOHN E., I. LEONARD, J. REID, J. CROW. *An Outline History of Spanish American Literature.* New York: Appleton-Century-Crofts, 1965. Pp. 127–28; 53–61. Gives pertinent historical and literary background of the period from Independence to Mexican Revolution.

GARCÍA CALDERÓN, VENTURA. *Del romanticismo al modernismo, Prosistas y poetas peruanos.* Paris: Librería Ollendorff, 1910. Pp. 254–79, selections of Chocano's poems; pp. 206–18, discussion of epic poetry in Peru and Chocano as epic poet; pp. iii–xvi, good discussion of literary periods in Peru, especially Romanticism through Modernism.

———. *Semblanzas de América*. Madrid: Cervantes, 1920? Pp. 109–23, perceptive discussion of Chocano's work.

GARCÍA PRADA, CARLOS. *Poetas modernistas hispanoamericanos*. Madrid: Ediciones Cultura Hispánica, 1956. Pp. 301–17; 7–29. Very fine discussion of Modernism, interesting personal opinions often shaded differently from accepted views. Unfavorable to Chocano.

GOLDBERG, ISAAC. *Studies in Spanish-American Literature*. New York: Brentano's, 1920. Chap. IV, pp. 246–95. Penetrating and comprehensive study of Chocano's work through *¡Fiat Lux!* Reflects high esteem in which poetry was held in that era. Pp. 367–71, literal translations of lines from poetry. Chap. I, pp. 1–100, discusses Modernism.

HESPELT, E. HERMAN, I. LEONARD, J. REID, J. CROW, J. ENGLEKIRK. *An Anthology of Spanish American Literature*. New York: Appleton-Century-Crofts, 1946. Pp. 540–56, brief introduction and selection of Chocano's poems.

MARIÁTEGUI, JOSÉ CARLOS. *Siete ensayos de interpretación de la realidad peruana*. Lima: Amauta, 1928. Pp. 200–204. Excellent essay on Peruvian Realism and the Indian situation; opinion of Chocano's place in Peruvian literature.

MEZA FUENTES, ROBERTO. "La poesía de José Santos Chocano," *Nosotros*, LXXVIII (1934), 286–311. Valuable discussion, especially the comparison between Chocano's early and last works.

RODRÍGUEZ-PERALTA, PHYLLIS. "The Peru of Chocano and Vallejo," *Hispania*, XLIV (December, 1961), 635–42. Comparison of the work of these two Peruvian poets. Considers the impact of two different environments within Peru.

SÁNCHEZ, LUIS ALBERTO, *Aladino, o, vida y obra de José Santos Chocano*. Mexico: Libro-Mex, 1960. Extensive study of the poet.

———. "Chocano, traductor," *Revista Iberoamericana*, XXIII (January–June, 1958), 113–19. Rambling account of circumstances surrounding Chocano's translation of Brazilian poet's work.

———. *La literatura peruana*. Lima: Edit. P.T.C.M., 1946. Pp. 46–59. Survey of Peruvian literature; refers to the influence of nature.

TAMAYO VARGAS, AUGUSTO. *Literatura peruana*. Tomo II. Lima: Universidad Nacional Mayor de San Marcos, 1965. Pp. 586–605, comprehensive critique which considers various aspects of Chocano's poetic development.

TORRES-RÍOSECO, ARTURO. *Ensayos sobre literatura latinoamericana*. Berkeley: Univ. of California Press, 1953. Pp. 172–80. Discerning essay on Chocano and his place in Spanish American literature.

UMPHREY, GEORGE. "José Santos Chocano, 'el Poeta de América',"
Hispania, III (December, 1920), 304–15. Principally a comparison
of Chocano and Whitman. Translated and widely read in Spanish
America.
University of Missouri Studies. See Translations.

Index